N.D.P

BERLITZ®

D0656609

DORDOGNE

- A ✓ in the text denotes a highly recommended sight
- A complete A–Z of practical information starts on p. 116
- Extensive mapping throughout: on cover flaps and in text

Printed in Switzerland by Weber SA, Bienne.

First edition (1993/1994)

Although we make every effort to ensure the accuracy of the information in this guide, changes do occur. If you have any new information, suggestions or corrections to contribute, we would like to hear from you. Please write to Berlitz Publishing at the above address.

Text:	Giles Allen
Staff editors:	Kathryn-Jane Müller-Griffiths, Sarah Hudson
Photography:	Jürg Donatsch
Cartography:	Micro Map
Layout:	Cristina Silva
Thanks to:	Winifred Allen, Adam T. Cooper, Louise Caroline Facer, Marie-Paule and Olivia Séïté for their invaluable assistance in the preparation of this guide.

CONTENTS

The Dordogne and its Inhabitants

Here, in a nutshell of a province, is the quintessence of France – good living, culture, history and gastronomy. Blessed with a temperate climate, a landscape as green as the Garden of Eden and rivers that irrigate a bountiful land, the Dordogne lives in perfect equilibrium. A population that allies southern exuberance with northern rationality and a cuisine that is the envy of the world add the finishing touches to a perfect holiday.

The British refer to the area as the Dordogne, its formal *département* name The French, however, with their customary disregard for administrative niceties, stick firmly to the original name, the Périgord. The Dordogne *département* covers approximately the same area as the Périgord, and falls within the province of Aquitaine (capital Bordeaux).

Walnuts, mushrooms, truffles, geese and ducks galore, as well as a plentiful supply of fruit and vegetables bear witness to the region's self-sufficiency in food. A thousand-and-one castles, châteaux, manors and fortresses (even humble farmhouses boast turrets) dot the countryside, occupying every cliff top, lording over every hamlet and basking beside every turn in the river. The Dordogne, even in the height of summer, clings to its image of bucolic serenity.

It's hardly surprising that large numbers of stressed town folk make a beeline for the tranquillity found in the Dordogne. The British have come in droves and many have even settled here permanently. Two million annual visitors are expected by the year 2 000.

On the surface, everything looks bright – so bright that it comes as a shock to learn that the Dordogne has been an impoverished province. Even today, its country population is ageing and rapidly deserting the villages for a 'better' life in the city.

Its apparent serenity is an illusion, of course, as it always was – life has been a constant struggle, against the Vikings, the English, Albigensian 'heretics', Protestant Reformers and Catholic dogmatists, as well as feudal lords (or simply crippling taxes). Skirmishes announcing the Hundred Years' War started here over 100 years *before* the war 'officially' broke out, and religious strife afterwards caused untold misery. However, during these bitter conflicts, fortresses, castles and churches continued to be built. Each time man went a step further in his search for beauty, thus creating a landscape so perfect and harmonious that one wonders whether the châteaux existed from time immemorial.

But the Dordogne really begins with the River.

From the river's source way up in the mountains of the Auvergne, it trickles down, swelling here, narrowing there, gushing or lazing its way over 483 km (300 miles), until it starts its playful, meandering course towards its junction with the Garonne and the Atlantic beyond. Other rivers converge with the Dordogne, the Vézère in particular, adding their own special charm to the Dordogne's majesty.

Owing to the unique combination of abundant fish supplies and dwellings safe from the wild animals in the myriad caves and grottoes riddling the valley cliffs, more traces of man's presence thousands of years ago have been found

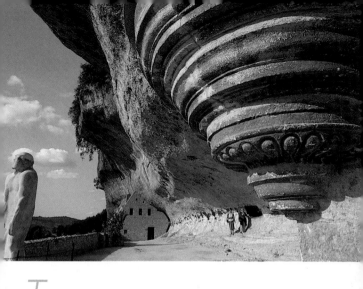

Timeless La Roque-Gageac with its château is built into a cliff overhanging the Dordogne while Dardé's primitive Neanderthal man (not Cro-Magnon; he'd be offended) surveys the scene from Les Eyzies.

here than anywhere else in France. Around Les Eyzies-de-Tayac, more than half the major French Palaeolithic finds and wall paintings came to light; for man could use the natural caves, cavities and the overhanging rocks along the Vézère, the Isle and Dronne rivers for shelter or as sanctuaries. He created works of art of such force and beauty 15,000–20,000 years ago that they still astound us today.

In the triangle formed by the Vézère and the Dordogne rivers lie many of the treasures that make the Dordogne so attractive: its most prestigious caves (the 'original' Lascaux, Font-de-Gaume, Les Combarelles, etc.), its mightiest fortresses **7**

(Beynac and Castelnaud), its prettiest villages (Domme, La Roque-Gageac and Les Eyzies), and châteaux galore (Fénelon, Puymartin and Montfort among countless others), not forgetting Sarlat, totally preserved from the ravages of time, morally if not technically the capital of the Dordogne.

You shouldn't be confined to the Dordogne *département* (the third largest in France) – the Lot (formerly called the Quercy) and Corrèze, to the north and east respectively, are equally enchanting. Don't miss Collonges-la-Rouge, a village built entirely of red sandstone. Nearby Souillac and historic Martel are worth a visit, too. Rocamadour, constructed onto a vertical wall of rock, was among the indispensable pilgrimages for any good Christian in the Middle Ages. Neighbouring Padirac is Europe's most impressive cave, of cathedral-like proportions. Many call Saint-Cirq-Lapopie the prettiest village in France, while the 17,000-

*P*eace and tranquillity reigns throughout the Dordogne, where village life is calm and unhurried.

year-old cave drawings at Pech-Merle are among the most moving examples of Palaeolithic art.

If cultural aspects are important in a holiday, so, too, are sports and outdoor activities. Here the Dordogne can offer an impressive variety: the finest canoeing, fishing, horse-riding, hiking and cycling, not to mention tennis

and swimming. The leisure parks and attractions for adults and children range from reptile or monkey parks at Rocamadour to pony rides and boat trips down the Dordogne. In the evenings, *son et lumière* shows enliven many a château's history. Theatre comes into its own at the Sarlat festival while music festivals abound in such settings as Saint-Amand-de-Coly, Brantôme, Bergerac and Bonaguil.

On rainy days, museums cater to all interests: truffles at Sorges, butterflies at Rocamadour, prehistory at Les Eyzies, tobacco at Bergerac... Châteaux also make entertaining and instructive outings, especially for the children: from Montaigne's spartan library where the philosopher sought peace to Castelnaud's museum on war techniques in the Middle Ages. There is never a shortage of activities; let your mood dictate.

Many a pleasant moment is likely to be spent either sipping an apéritif on a terrace or eating some of the best meals you're ever likely to taste in dream-like surroundings. *Foie gras*, to be accompanied by a glass of Monbazillac, is found on most menus; *confit de canard*, duck stewed in its own fat for hours, is a pure gastronomic delight. If you think you know good omelettes, you may well be astounded by the *omelette aux cèpes* (with boletus mushrooms). The standard of cuisine is superior to most other regions of France; however, the Dordogne clings jealously to its reputation and remains reasonably priced.

If you're guaranteed to take gastronomic souvenirs away with you, you are also bound to harbour unforgettable visual and emotional recollections, be it the wisps of mist rising from the Dordogne as it awakes each morning or the sun setting on the mellow houses and verdant valleys of a timeless village. But in the end it is the total experience, the warmth of the welcome, the charm of what man created and the beauty of nature that form this delightful province which makes you want to return, year after year.

A Brief History

PREHISTORIC TIMES

In 1884, at Cro-magnon, just outside Les Eyzies-de-Tayac, five skeletons of the upper Palaeolithic age were discovered. The missing link had at last been found between prehistoric man and ourselves and a new science, prehistory, was born. Many unsolved riddles remain, but little by little the full picture of man's evolution is emerging – thanks largely to discoveries in the Dordogne.

Neanderthal man, Cro-magnon's predecessor and direct

A reconstruction of Neanderthal man's first dwellings of animal bones at Le Thot. Similar types of habitat have been found in Siberia.

ancestor, was discovered in a valley in Germany in the mid-19th century. He was a *Homo sapiens*, literally 'a man who knows'; but Cro-magnon was what the anthropologists call a *Homo sapiens sapiens*, 'a man who knows he knows'. The Neanderthal man developed very slowly, with a skull shaped somewhat differently from our own, but by 30,000–20,000 BC our Cro-magnon ancestor was identical to ourselves in appearance and had started to make use of the natural caves and shelters along the Dordogne.

Wall paintings and engravings from the Magdalenian era (from c. 17,000–9,000 BC) depict a fantastic array of animals: the mammoth (found at Rouffignac and Lascaux), the bison and reindeer (Font-de-Gaume), the wolf and fox (Limeuil), the horse (most caves), the bison (Pech-Merle, among others) and even imaginary animals such as the unicorn at Lascaux. The representation of the animals Cro-magnon man and his descendants drew doubtless served some ritual purpose as art and magic were mysteriously linked.

After the creative millennia of the Magdalenian period, there was an artistic decline. However, hunting objects, harpoons and arrows carved from bone or stone, now in the museum of Les Eyzies, became more plentiful as time progressed; so did funereal sites and tombs. Jewellery and sculpted figures, such as the *vénus*, particularly the *Vénus à la corn*, started to appear. The first signs of cultivation, however, only date from 4,000 BC; shortly afterwards, the raising of sheep, goats and cattle began. Gradually groups formed and settled in villages.

THE GAULS AND GALLO-ROMANS

Celtic peoples swept into Aquitaine from the East from the beginning of the 3rd century BC. Urban centres grew up, with tribal populations such as the Petrucores (who gave the Périgord its name) trading with the Romans in the province of Narbonne. However, the Romans decided to take over the area by force and the Petrucores-Gauls were no match for the might of Rome. The tribes of the south-west were rapidly absorbed into Roman society. Indeed, the province of Aquitaine, founded by the Romans in 16 BC, held together in spite of the barbarian invasions until the 4th century AD.

The capital of the area was the splendid Vesunna (Péri-gueux). The Romans introduced one particular novelty: the vine, and soon the local people dropped their Celtic beer and beat the Romans at their own game.

Peace and contentment were not to last: raids by the Goths between 230 and 280 AD inflicted great destruction, culminating in the disastrous year 406 when the Goths devastated Vesunna before heading on to Spain.

CHRISTIANITY

Largely through the church, Aquitaine retained some aspects of the structure inherited from the Gallo-Romans throughout the troubled times of the Visigoth and Vandal invasions. The church took over from the disintegrating Roman administration and managed the area during the long Dark Ages. Clovis and his Franks chased out the Visigoths in 507 at the battle of Vouillé, with the active support of the church hierarchy. Charlemagne made Aquitaine a kingdom in 778 but the province became a bone of contention. Then a new scourge appeared: the Normans, sailing up the main rivers, spreading terror and destruction wherever they went. The church organized resistance, growing stronger as the situation worsened.

ENTER THE ENGLISH

In 1058, or when William the Conqueror was setting off to conquer England, the future Duke Guillaume VIII, by a mixture of intrigue and impudence, had Gascony linked to Aquitaine, thereby creating a sizeable territory that ran from Poitiers and below the Loire **13**

Valley all the way down to the Pyrenees. Almost a century later, his descendant Duke William X died on the pilgrimage to Santiago de Compostela and left his daughter Eleanor in the care of the French King, Louis VI, who married her to his son, Louis le Jeune, in 1153.

This proved to be one of the capital events in the whole of French history, for Louis was austere and reflective, Eleanor flighty and hot-headed. The stormy marriage ended 15 years later. Eleanor reclaimed her property and promptly married Henry Plantagenet, Duke of Normandy and Count of Anjou, future King Henry II of England. Henry and Eleanor then owned much of France. Thus, with interruptions and fluctuating frontiers, Aquitaine became English 'territory' for the next 300 years. This did not change people's lives much to begin with: the Anglo-Gascon princes set up a solid administration to run the province, the personnel was recruited locally

The stunning site of Rocamadour shouldn't distract you from the 15th-century frescoes on Nôtre-Dame Chapel. The church tympanum at lovely Cavennac is as finely sculpted as a jewel.

and the language used was essentially Gascon or Latin. The problems that arose mostly concerned rivalries between leaders. From the 13th century onwards, squabbles centred around the question of whom Aquitaine was to pay homage to, a dispute that grew increasingly bitter until Edward claimed the throne of France itself, thereby sparking off the Hundred Years' War, which began in Aquitaine in 1337.

100 YEARS OF MISERY

Though it was not a continuous war, there was scarcely a part of Aquitaine or the Dordogne that did not suffer. Wanton cruelty (on both sides) and marauding bands, not to mention starvation and natural dis-

asters, brought the beautiful province to its knees. Edward III of England and his son, the Black Prince, initially gained the upper hand after the victory at Poitiers. At the Treaty of Brétigny, in 1360, they won complete control of Aquitaine (Edward giving up his claim to the throne in exchange for the whole of south-west France), but the French re-conquest steadily gained momentum. At Castillon in 1453, just outside Bergerac, Talbot and the English forces were defeated and **15**

Aquitaine was incorporated into the kingdom of France.

During these difficult years, a significant population increase encouraged many to leave town to farm virgin territories. Ecclesiastical vocations were on the increase; monks cleared land and built monasteries like Cadouin, which in turn attracted rural communities to till the soil and cater to the monks' needs. Meanwhile, the towns did not stand still, but developed around their cathedrals. The bourgeoisie undertook an ever bigger role in municipal affairs. Bordeaux's vineyards brought Aquitaine colossal wealth.

BUILDING SPREE

Various factors – economic growth, the population increase, the need to settle new areas, Anglo-French rivalry and military requirements – led to the creation of the *bastides*, new towns, built by both the French and English along a grid plan. Between 1246 and 1360, some 130 *bastides* were **16** constructed all over south-west France. In the Périgord they served as buffer towns on the borders between French and English zones of influence.

In this strife-ridden atmosphere, cathedral-building in the Dordogne never reached the heights of the Gothic masterpieces of northern France, nor did sculpting attain the exuberance of that of southern France. Yet the quantity of specifically Périgord Romanesque churches where military and religious functions merged (as at Saint-Amand-de-Coly) make up for this, while the sheer density and quality of châteaux is barely equalled anywhere.

These warlike times greatly encouraged the building of châteaux-fortresses: between the early Middle Ages and the 16th century, some 500 castles were built, renovated or rebuilt. They range from solid, imposing burgs such as Beynac and Castelnaud, and the 'baronies' like Biron, Bourdeilles and Bonaguil, to the more refined châteaux like those of the Loire, Jumilhac, Les Bories and Puyguilhem.

Castelnaud, occupied in turn by Cathars, English, Huguenots and Catholics, is everything a medieval castle should be.

RELIGIOUS STRIFE

Religious discontent throughout France grew more vociferous and the Reformation reached Aquitaine in 1532. Many members of the liberal professions of Sainte-Foy and Bergerac took up its cause, and the local Catholic clergy, feeling threatened, reacted. Persecution began, turning the Dordogne into a battlefield. Michel de Montaigne (1553–92), philosopher, twice mayor of Bordeaux, and a practising Catholic, tried preaching moderation to fanatics, but in vain. To make matters worse, unbearably heavy taxes were imposed. Between 1630 and 1675, townsfolk and *croquants* (as the local rebels were called) protested on various occasions, but to no avail. At the Revocation of the Edict of Nantes in 1685, many Huguenots, particularly in Bergerac, fled the country and, with famine and plagues also taking their toll, the Dordogne's population started to decrease.

The end of the Wars of Religion set a new building spree of churches and châteaux in motion, such as Hautefort, where the emphasis was on interior decoration. Imposing Renaissance buildings were also built in Sarlat and Périgueux, where Tourny, a dynamic Bordeaux town-planner, developed concepts of harmony and space in city planning.

Bordeaux, and the whole of Aquitaine, began to regain its former commercial importance in the 18th century by increasing the areas of its vineyards and by trading with overseas colonies. Monbazillac and Bergerac, with their Huguenot links to Holland, flourished again.

FALL AND RISE

The Revolution and the Continental Blockade of the French ports, however, reversed the trend, and Bordeaux – just as Aquitaine's 'inner core', the Périgord (re-baptised the Dordogne) – fell asleep, with an occasional brutal awakening as with the revolt of the *croquants* against the almost feudal lords. Rural emigration continued to increase and, without coal, the Dordogne was bypassed by the Industrial Revolution.

Although not a significant battle ground, the Dordogne paid a heavy tribute in lives during World War I. In the last war, the Germans razed Rouffignac, but otherwise the region survived more or less intact. It looked like the area was going to become an agricultural backwater until, with the discoveries of the Dordogne's extraordinary prehistoric remains and the phenomenon of tourism, the situation changed radically. While local reactions oscillate between the favourable and the hostile, the whole tourist movement is certainly contributing to the preservation of the Dordogne's beauty and to stemming the rural exodus.

Where to Go

To see the Dordogne properly within the space of a normal holiday is asking a great deal, unless you do everything at breakneck speed. It is better to sample the various types of sight – a couple of châteaux, caves and chasms, a museum and a market here or there, as well as a village of special interest. Intersperse your sightseeing with swimming breaks and picnics, shopping expeditions, plus a visit to a leisure park or garden. In this chapter we have selected the 'essentials', but the list is variable and *ad infinitum* according to taste.

In summer there are large numbers of people at the major sights, entailing long queues and occasional disappointment. For instance, you might have to wait *two* days to join a tour of Font-de-Gaume. In summer a tiny village like La Roque-Gageac, 'designed' for a maximum population of a hundred, swells to many times the number it can comfortably hold. It is often advisable to visit out of season or else early in the morning or in the late afternoon.

For a division of the sightseeing, we have followed the

Monpazier, most perfect of the bastide towns, basks in car-free peace.

*T*wo eternal aspects of the Dordogne; the riverside scenery (above) by the Vézère near La Madeleine, and (right) the place de la Liberté in medieval Sarlat, a market town and gourmets' delight.

Tourist Office's breakdown of the Périgord into four 'colours': White (*Blanc*) refers to the proud limestone cliffs around Périgueux and a band down the centre; Green (*Vert*) is the agricultural northern section; the south-western part of the province is called Purple (*Pour-* *pre*) because of its vineyards near Bergerac; and the Black Périgord (*Noir*), as green as green can be, is so called because its dense oak forests assume dark hues. To this we have added an 'excursion' section to some of the top sights of the Lot (Quercy) and Corrèze.

Périgord Noir

✓ SARLAT

A little market town of 10,000 inhabitants (that attracts a million visitors a year), set in a valley with a beautiful hilly backdrop, Sarlat was 'rediscovered' by André Malraux, Minister of Culture under de Gaulle and also, as so often

happens in France, a brilliant author and intellectual.

All that was here, golden-stoned town houses with pepper-pot turrets and heavy *lauze* or deep-red tile roofs, small alleyways and minute market places, has been carefully spruced up and renovated. Gas lamps for the streets were reintroduced and houses were allowed all mod cons, provided they did not detract from the

perfection of the exterior. The idea was not to create a 'museum' town, but a living, actively functioning centre within a medieval framework.

Split in two by the long **rue de la République**, both sides of the town should be visited in turn. The main square, the **place de la Liberté**, is an opera stage in itself, where cafés and restaurants give a relaxed air to the more formal 17th-century town hall. As so often in France, the Tourist Office occupies part of a historical monument, beside the **Hôtel de Vienne** or **Hôtel de Maleville**, part Italian, part French Renaissance in style.

The Tourist Office organizes two-hour English tours round the town; the hours are posted outside. Heading behind the Tourist Office, past 13th–16th-century half-timbered houses with the characteristic *lauze* tiling of the area, you'll instantly spot, on the corner of the place du Peyrou, the 16th-century **birthplace of Etienne de la Boétie** (a philosopher-poet who was a close friend of Montaigne), the most striking of the 16th-century Italian Renaissance houses in Sarlat (at that time Italy was all the rage).

Opposite, the **Cathédral de Saint-Sacerdos**, a Gothic structure built on a Romanesque base, is something of a hybrid. However, there are some lovely Italian Florid Gothic windows in the wing that was once the **Palais episcopal** (Bishopric). The curious **Jardin des Enfeus** (Garden of Funereal Niches), where Romanesque and Gothic tombs have been hacked out of the cliff face, leads via some steps to the mysterious, beautifully shaped **Lanterne des Morts** (Lantern of the Dead).

After a look at the 16th-century **Hôtel de Génis**, continue down the rue du Présidial to the rue Fénelon and back into the place de la Liberté. If the houses look serried, remember that within Sarlat's ramparts space was at a premium; openair stalls occupied the ground level while the rich lived on the floors above, providing themselves with balconies to obtain more light. Since taxes were calculated by ground space, it was a clever way of keeping them lower!

Back in place de la Liberté, go past the castle-like, hexagonal tower **Hôtel de Gisson** and the former church **Sainte-Marie**, whose playful gargoyles and amputated church tower lend it character. The church served as an ammunition dump and after the Revolution it was sold to a *marchand de biens*, who decided the chancel blocked his view and therefore removed it.

In the **rue des Consuls** the various grand town houses compete: most impressive is the **Hôtel Plamon** that belonged to rich cloth merchants trying to 'keep up with the Joneses'. New parts were added between the 14th and 17th centuries, providing a range of architectural styles. The corner of the street has a rounded overhanging balcony supported by a small arch, that helped the traffic squeeze by. The 15th-century **Hôtel de Vassal** with its double watchtower lies on the corner of the **marché aux oies** (goose market), a tiny enclave of a market, much used in film sets. Look inside the **Hôtel Tapinois de Betou** at the magnificent wooden 17th-century staircase, each part carved from a single log.

Y ou'll see him by the river at La Roque-Gageac; craftsmen of all kinds flourish hereabouts.

Over on the west side of the rue de la République, head up the **rue des Armes**. The dark narrow passageways have a more cut-throat air about them and restoration work is not so advanced as elsewhere.

Nevertheless, the beauty of the houses, the sculptural intricacies, the doorways (notice the amusing knockers) and windows provide as much fascination as the more 'elite' side of town.

The flowered balconies and old greystone houses with deep-red roofs bestow a unity of style on the fortified hillside town of Domme.

AROUND SARLAT

 The classic 30-odd km (19-mile) excursion from Sarlat takes a visitor along the Dordogne, beside the most beautiful, dramatic part of the river. Head towards the **Cingle de Montfort** (Montfort Meander), the first of a number of bends you'll meet as the river turns back on itself and hems in a slice of land. At one point, you'll have a stunning view of the **Château de Montfort**, which unfortunately cannot be visited. Cross the Dordogne and climb up through a fertile region to **Domme**, one of the greatest *bastides* due to its impregnable site.

Completely won over by the enormous dome-shaped rock (which explains the name 'Domme') overlooking the valley of the Dordogne, Philippe the Bold decided in 1280 to build a fortress to control all the converging routes. The stout walls around the city, with three intact gates, are still there. You'll probably enter by the fortified **Porte des Tours**, in which the Knights Templar were imprisoned between 1307 and 1318, scrawling their coded messages on the walls.

Domme deserves a thorough visit. It is packed with 15th–18th-century houses in *carreyrous (*narrow alleyways), with a unique unity of style and purpose. The view from the esplanade over the slim Dordogne towards the château of Montfort perched on its spur is majestic. Walk around the ramparts to the **Belvédère de la Barre**. The sturdy church just beside the gardens was partially destroyed by the Huguenot leader Geoffroy de Vivans in 1589, who took some of the stones to build defences. De Vivans, frustrated after three attempts at taking the *bastide*, scaled the cliff to break into the virtually unassailable bastion.

Domme's roughly triangular form begins at the top of the hill and tapers down to the ruins of the Château du Roi at the bottom. The main square, the **place des Gouverneurs**, not only contains the Tourist Office, housed in the curiously shaped **Maison des Gouverneurs**, but also the **covered 25** market (*halles*), with a most unusual flowered wooden terrace supported on massive stone pillars. Below lies the entrance to the **grottoes**, 450 m (1,476 ft) long, a perfect refuge for villagers during attacks. The grottoes' forest of crystal formations is illuminated during the 25-minute visit with ultra-violet-light effects bringing out all their sparkle. In **La Martine Grotto**, prehistoric paintings of bison and ibex were discovered in 1963 along with remains of mammoth (teeth, bones and tusks – approximately 30,000 years old). Some of these have stayed on the site but most are displayed in the nearby **Musée d'Art et de Tradition populaire**.

La Roque-Gageac is said to be the third most visited spot in France after the Mont-Saint-Michel and Rocamadour. This miniscule village seems to be glued to the rock face, hemmed in at its feet by the languorous Dordogne. The village's site below an oak-tree-cloaked cliff, its unity of colour and style, its serried rank of neat honey-coloured houses (mainly restaurants today) and its small refined 16th-century **Manoir de Tarde** makes it all incredibly picturesque. From the little 1709 chapel that hangs between earth and sky, gaze down on the *gabares* (barges) idling down the Dordogne and at the powerful but magical Château

*U*sing the sheer rockface, La Roque-Gageac gets its charm from being built right into the cliff.

de Castelnaud seated squarely on the hill opposite.

Only a few miles separates La Roque-Gageac from **Beynac-et-Cazenac**. Way up above its village, perched on one of the most beautiful ridges in the whole Dordogne valley, lies the castle (it's a 3-km/2-mile drive winding past tobacco fields and vineyards). Although it may appear austere from afar, when you see the reflection in the blue-green waters of the Dordogne and the sun shimmering on its stone walls, all apparent severity vanishes.

This eagle's nest is not only a castle, but a mini-village set within the walls of a castle. Richard the Lion-Heart gave the original fortress to one of his lieutenants, but the 13th-century barons of Beynac built it into something resembling what we see today. During the Hundred Years' War, the River Dordogne constituted the dividing line between English and French territories and Beynac found itself within the French orbit. During the Wars of Religion, the lords of Beynac took up the Catholic cause,

helping wipe out the Huguenot army at Vergt in 1562, but nevertheless converted to Protestantism in 1575. They changed back again in 1687. Such were the times!

Two walls surround the castle on its vulnerable side, the plateau; on the other side, a sheer drop of 150 m (492 ft) down to the Dordogne made it impregnable. Inside, the main building is roughly square, with a bastion running right along the rocky spur that plunges precipitously down to the village. An austere dungeon gives the final medieval touch (13th century), while the main 13th–14th-century building is extended by a 15th-century manor house.

Not only was the **Château de Castelnaud** on the other side of the River Dordogne from Beynac, it was also on the 'other side' in the Hundred Years' War. This English stronghold was an arch-rival in every sense: strategically well-sited and just as strong and well-equipped as its counterpart. Even today it battles with Beynac for attention.

27

In 1214 Simon de Montfort destroyed much of the original fortress but built an even more powerful castle. During the Hundred Years' War, the two powerful castles struggled implacably to control the Dordogne. At the end of the Hundred Years' War, in a forlorn state, with only keep and curtain wall in their original state, Castlenaud was rebuilt by Brandelis de Caumont.

The age of the fortress, however, was drawing to an end; the new age was looking for more pleasure-orientated and less warlike homes, so the Caumonts moved over to the Château Les Milandes nearby (see below), more in the style of the fashionable Loire châteaux. Castelnaud's fortress was 'lent' to the Huguenot de Vivans during the Wars of Religion. He adapted the castle to the conditions of the age and added further fortifications. The château was soon abandoned and used as a stone quarry after the French Revolution, with undergrowth sprouting from the walls. Then in 1967, when its value was again recognized, restoration work on a grandiose scale began. And what better castle could have been chosen to house the **Musée de la Guerre au Moyen-Age** (Medieval Warfare Museum)?

Apart from interesting video films, full-sized catapults, slings that could project 20–50-kg (44–110-lb) missiles up to 180 m (590 ft), crossbows and models of every kind of devilish invention, there's a mass of primitive cannons, stone cannon balls, vicious axes, maces, lances and halberds. The young will enjoy the room full of computer games, books and comics about the Middle Ages.

For a taste of more gentle living, we now head towards Les Milandes, the 'second residence' of the Caumonts. Today **Les Milandes** owes its celebrity to Josephine Baker who chose the château to fulfill her dream of a 'world village'. Bringing together orphans of all creeds, colours and nationalities, she set out to create a spirit of mutual understanding. Her personality still pervades the château, a model of harmo-

ymbolizing the Dordogne Valley, Beynac Castle is serenely mirrored in the river, while the village huddles beneath. The well-restored castle compound was brilliantly conceived to fend off attacks.

ny that merges Gothic and Renaissance styles. Built in 1489, it remained in the Caumont family until the Revolution.

Belvès is an old medieval city at an important crossroads sitting on a spur of a hill. The seven towers, including the sinister dungeon and the 15th-century churches, its old streets and refined aristocratic *hôtels* give the town style, while the covered market with superb timberwork in the central round square, **place d'Armes**, lends animation. On one of the wooden pillars supporting the covered market is a cast-iron chain of the pillory used up until the Revolution. **29**

PREHISTORIC PÉRIGORD

The River Dordogne certainly wins hands down in the beautiful châteaux stakes; the Vézère, however, takes the lion's share when it comes to prehistory – and scenic views.

Caves and grottoes can be categorized schematically into three sorts: those with prehistoric paintings and engravings, those of 'mineral' rather than historical interest and the *abris,* troglodyte dwellings or shelters, many medieval.

For most visits a guide is obligatory and the hours of each tour fixed: usually a blessing in disguise as the guides – often young, enthusiastic graduates – will add anecdotes and conjectures to enliven a science as yet in its infancy.

Three golden rules apply to all caves and grottoes: do not touch the walls on any account, do not take photographs and do not smoke. Caves are, contrary to what one might imagine, fragile.

Where do we start? Best in **Les Eyzies-de-Tayac** itself, an attractive village spread out below cliffs as the River Vézère loops round and meets up with the little River Beune.

Man has been living in the area for something like 70,000 years (give or take a few millennia). Magdalenian remains (roughly 19,000 BC) lie beside medieval troglodytic ruins, thus making Les Eyzies an amazing time machine.

For the layman, the problem is how to relate the scientific name (mostly taken from the villages in this area where finds were made) to the development of man. Luckily, on the spot and built into the cliff side is France's foremost prehistoric museum, the **Musée National de la Préhistoire**, an outstanding exhibition of the evolution of primitive man to the present day. Exhibits here range from the stone arms of Abbevillian man (300,000 years ago) to the Périgordian (35,000 to 20,000 BC), who worked bone and created jewellery, on to the Magdalenian (19,000 to 9,000 BC), who invented the harpoon and fishhook.

31

Prehistoric Résumé

There are so many caves and grottoes around you'll need to make a choice. Here in a nutshell are those within easy reach of Les Eyzies and Sarlat, with distances from Les Eyzies or the nearest town, content and telephone number. Check opening times on the spot – they're constantly changing and different in high/low season.

Abri du Cap Blanc (painting/sculpture). 6 km (4 miles) near Tamniès. Tel. 53 59 21 74. Open Mar. to Oct.

Abri Pataud. In Les Eyzies. Museum on site of excavations. Tel. 53 06 92 46. Open all year. Closed Mon. in low season.

Carpe-Diem (crystal formations). 4 km (2.5 miles) near Manaurie. Tel. 53 06 93 63. Open every day Mar. to mid Sept.

Castel Merle (deposits, excavations, prehistoric shelter, paintings, engravings). 14 km (9 miles) near Sergeac. Tel. 53 50 77 76. Open every day mid-June to mid-Sept. Groups by appointment all year.

Les Cent Mammouths, Rouffignac (paintings/engravings). 14 km (9 miles) on the road to Rouffignac. Tel. 53 05 41 71. Open Easter to end Oct.

Centre d'Art Préhistorique du Thot (museum/park of prehistory). 20 km (12.5 miles) near Montignac. Tel. 53 53 44 35. Open Feb. to Dec. Tickets at the *Syndicat d'Initiative* in Montignac. Same ticket valid for *Lascaux II*.

Gisement de Régourdou (prehistoric field, museum, bear burial ground). 1 km (0.5 mile) from Lascaux II. Tel. 53 51 81 23 . Open all year.

Gouffre de Proumeyssac (chasm, crystal formations). 15 km (9.5 miles) near Le Bugue. Tel. 53 07 27 47. Open every day from April school holidays till Nov 11. Easy access for elderly or handicapped persons. Annual closing in Jan.

Grotte de Bara Bahau (engravings). 10 km (6 miles) near Le Bugue. Tel. 53 07 27 47. Open every day from April school holidays till Nov 11. Easy access for elderly or handicapped persons. Annual closing Nov 12 to Jan 31. Visit:35 minutes.

Grotte des Combarelles (engravings). 2 km (1.25 miles) just outside Les Eyzies. Tel. 53 06 97 72. Open all year. Closed Wed.

Grotte de Font-de-Gaume (paintings). 1 km (0.5 mile) just outside Les Eyzies. Tel. 53 06 97 48. Open all year. Closed Tues.

Grotte du Grand Roc (geological formations). 1.5 km (1 mile) just outside Les Eyzies. Tel. 53 06 96 76. Open Mar. to Nov. Visit: 30 minutes.

Grotte de Villars (rock formations/paintings). 12 km (7.5 miles) from Brantôme. Tel. 53 54 82 36. Open Jun. to mid-Sept.

Lascaux II (facsimile of most outstanding cave paintings of original Lascaux cave). 2 km (1.25 miles) from Montignac. Tel. 53 53 44 35. Open Feb. to Dec. Tickets *only* from the *Syndicat d'Initiative* in Montignac in July/Aug. Same ticket valid for entry to *Le Thot* – not dated.

Laugerie Basse (deposits and museum). 1.5 km (1 mile) just outside Les Eyzies. Tel. 53 06 97 12. Open May to Sept.

Laugerie Haute (prehistoric deposits). 2 km (1.25 miles) just outside Les Eyzies. Tel. 53 06 97 48. By appointment. Contact *Font-de-Gaume.*

Village Troglodytique de La Madeleine (troglodyte village,15th-century chapel). 8 km (5 miles) near Tursac. Tel. 53 06 92 49. Open every day mid-Feb. to end Nov.

Village Troglodytique de La Roque Saint-Christophe (troglodyte city). 10 km (6 miles) near Tursac. Tel. 53 50 70 45. Open every day end Mar. to mid-Nov.

TOP SIGHTS

While everyone has their preferences, two Palaeolithic sites stand out as particularly interesting: Font-de-Gaume (maximum number of visitors permitted: 340 a day) and Les Combarelles (six visitors at a time with the guide) – but go now while you still can. In spite of draconian anti-pollution measures, it is still possible that these caves, like Lascaux and Altamira in Spain, will have to be closed to the public for their preservation. The thrill of seeing the originals on the spot is irreplaceable.

Font-de-Gaume's cave has been visited by man for centuries, as we know from the graffiti scrawled on top of the paintings (one is dated 1854). It's a 400-m (1,312-ft) climb from the road to the narrow entrance of the cave that burrows back 125 m (410 ft), with cavities running off at various points. The cave was already fossilized 50,000 years ago and the only alteration carried out is the clay floor that has been lowered for visitors.

The first drawings (of bison, horses, mammoth, deer and oxen, even rhinoceroses) dating from 12,000 BC start after 50 m (164 ft) down the narrow

Countless generations of man lived at La Roque St-Christophe, building a five-floor town into the rock. At Le Thot (right) you can see examples of early cave life.

so-called 'Rubicon' passage (it widens later). With a torch the guide will point out the admirable design and draughtsmanship of these 'primitive' artists and their use of the contours of the rock to make the paintings three-dimensional. Painted by the flickering light of an oil lamp, artists crouching or on their knees (or for the taller parts on a fairly basic form of scaffolding) produced drawings that bear an undeniable affinity with the works of great modern artists like Picasso. The culminating frieze of four bison, the so-called *Chapelle aux bisons* in brown on the white calcite rock, is spellbinding.

Horses take pride of place in **Les Combarelles** – there are at least 140. At ground level, you penetrate some 150 m (492 ft) into this cave before meeting the first engravings, that carry on for another 135 m

(443 ft). To the naked eye, they are not always easy to distinguish: many are superimposed and follow the contours of the rock. Some 300 animals (others claim 800) have so far been discerned – bears, bison, reindeer and mammoth engraved in all kinds of positions on the walls spring to life before us, created by artists standing at this very same spot some 12,000 to 10,000 BC. Unlike most caves, there are some 48 human figures represented, admittedly not very lifelike, and a most unusual lioness and an ibex, as well as a reindeer drinking. Paintings here are rarer than at Font-de-Gaume, finished and unfinished engravings plentiful.

Stone-Age Art

As no household tools or weapons were found near the paintings of the deep galleries, scholars have deduced that most of the French caves were not dwellings but sanctuaries where stone-age man depicted the beasts he hunted and probably worshipped. For his home, he preferred cave entrances, the shelter of a cliff overhang or primitive wig-wam-style tents, where mammoth bones and reindeer skins served as tenting. Some of the frescoes show animals pierced with arrows and spears, perhaps a form of magic to promote success in the hunt.

The artists were past masters at using the forms of the rock surfaces they chose to help obtain three-dimensional effects and to give the subject matter relief or movement.

They depicted their potential game with red and yellow oxidized iron, powdered ochre, black charcoal and animal fats. Sometimes they used their fingers or worked with stencils, or dabbed on the paint with tufts of hair. Otherwise they blew powdered colour on to the walls through hollow bones or vegetable stalks, basically the same technique as aerosol-graffiti artists in the latter-day caves of a modern subway.

To reach the charming hamlet of La Madeleine, you pass through **Tursac,** where you'll notice the warm tones of the Romanesque church and its outsize bell tower and the **Préhisto-Parc,** that provides a graphic reconstruction of life in prehistoric times.

La Madeleine is first and foremost an extraordinary site – a thin slice of land on a narrow rocky promontory where the Vézère loops back on itself. Down by the riverside, beneath the overhanging ledges of the rock, the first Palaeolithic deposits were discovered, thus giving the name Magdalenian to this age and culture. For nearly 4,000 years (from about 12,000 to 8,000 BC), prehistoric man settled here, leaving traces of his daily life: flint and bone artefacts, animal remains from his hunts, art objects and even burial tombs. For nearly a century excavations have been going on, and shortly the site will be opened to the public.

Rising vertically above the Vézère, some 80 m (262 ft) along is **La Roque Saint Christophe,** a white cliff half a mile long. Like a massive apartment block, five stories high, honeycombed with perhaps a hundred *cluzeaux* (small natural dugouts or lookout caves), this rock provided shelter for countless generations of men of different ages. The earliest were probably of the Mousterian era. The immense natural shelter was probably successively lived in by Cro-magnon man, during the Neolithic Age, the Bronze Age (around 1,500 BC), the Iron Age (approximately 800 BC), in Gallo-Roman times, in the Dark Ages and finally the Middle Ages. The ruins and remains visible date mostly from those latter times.

Montignac is a likeable enough town in its own right, but its real attraction is as a departure point for the world-famous caves at **Lascaux,** a mile or so away. For Lascaux represents an amazing moment in human history: the birth of art.

Although the opening to the original cave was visible, the porch caved in at some point **37**

*F*or millennia, mammoths were at home in the Dordogne. Now a reproduction trumpets at Le Thot.

ly distinguishable galleries. Executed around 17,000 BC, the 1,500 representations, either engraved or painted, of aurochs, bulls and cows, horses and reindeer, ibex and bison, symbols and combs, provide an awe-inspiring spectacle as you advance from 'room' to 'room'.

The *real* caves are practically closed to the general public (five visitors a day, usually students of prehistory). Pollution threatened to destroy them, so that they were blocked off in the interests of preserving this world treasure for humanity. In quantity and quality of prehistoric drawings, nothing to match Lascaux has yet been unearthed. Lascaux' fame spread quickly and after a million visitors between 1948 and 1963 the caves had suffered far more than in the tens of thousands of years that preceded them. The rock inside was 'sick'.

But, so as not to deprive the public of its heritage, a perfect facsimile, **Lascaux II**, was installed in 1983 two hundred yards (180m) from the original site. In high season the tickets

and concealed it, miraculously preserving it from atmospheric pollution. In September 1940, four young boys chasing their dog after it had slipped down a hole were spellbound by what they saw by the faint light of a torch. The original cave bore in about 150 m (492 ft) into the **38** limestone rock with four, clear-

for Lascaux II must be obtained at the Tourist Office in Montignac, from 9 a.m. onwards. Queues, even for the replica, can be long and tours leave on the dot. They move fast (the visit lasts only half an hour), so try and take it all in rapidly by doing a bit of homework to begin with (or visit Le Thot first, see below).

Complement your visit of Lascaux with a side trip to **Le Thot**, 6 km (4 miles) away, a centre of prehistory. Some excellent exhibits, charts and models do a lot to help put everything into perspective. You've paid for your visit with your ticket to Lascaux II, and the film of the making of the Lascaux facsimile is fascinating.

Overlooking the Vézère stands the dreamy white **Château de Losse** (only open in July/August); the Italian Renaissance furniture and Flemish 17th-century tapestries inside definitely deserve a visit. Take a look at it from the other side of the river, too, on your way

Stone Walling

Wall painting took off around the Aurignacian age 30,000 BC, at about the time when Cro-magnon man 'replaced' Neanderthal. From its beginnings to the moment it apparently declined around 9,000 BC, this art form flourished within a clearly delineated geographical area that ran from the Urals to the Atlantic (suggesting that the peoples arrived from the east), and the subjects depicted everywhere covered more or less the same themes, of animals and hunting scenes. It reached its heyday between about 17,000 and 10,000 BC in south-western France and northern Spain. To talk of a prehistoric 'civilization' with similar social, even political organization throughout the area would be to assume perhaps too much, but the artists did all use the same techniques and probably had similar rites. All the rest is conjecture.

to Sergeac (see p. 41). From this vantage point you can admire the elegant terrace-balustrade slotting so perfectly into the overhanging cliff.

The Périgord is full of Romanesque churches, but few match the graceful **Saint-Léon-sur-Vézère**. Surrounded by trees and mirrored in the Vézère that passes right beside it, the town's 11th-century church, with its stone-slabbed (*lauze*) roof and square bell tower with three radiating domed chapels beneath it, is a wonderful example of the harmony of Périgord Romanesque. Inside, the rounded vaults seem to arch beneath the weight and grow outwards. Beautifully restored, the regular summer music festivals could hardly find a more fitting setting than Saint-Léon's interior.

Jacquou, Robin Hood of the Dordogne

Jacquou le Croquant may be a fictitious character from the imagination of a local writer, Eugène Le Roy, but his adventures and sufferings are based on 19th-century Périgord. Le Roy, a tax collector by profession, tells the story of Jacquou who led a popular uprising (the so-called *croquants*) against the Comte de Nansac, the cruel and extortionate lord of the local château, l'Herm. Jacquou's father kills the brutal estate controller and dies a galley-slave. His mother expires shortly afterwards in dire poverty, forcing Jacquou to swear revenge. Jacquou was taken in by the Abbé Bonal in Fanlac and given some instruction. Thrown into jail at l'Herm, falsely accused of poaching, Jacquou is finally freed and incites the peasants to revolt. The château with all in it are burned. Jacquou is saved by the Revolution of 1830 and freed, and lives more or less happily ever after. After the television film, many a warm tear was shed, particularly in the Dordogne. So true does the story ring, many local people today claim descent from their own Robin Hood.

Sergeac has many interesting features, including the picturesque village itself and its breathtaking view of the Vézère. As you arrive, note the highly unusual **croix hosannière** (Hosanna Cross) at the crossroads, sculpted with a knight with a salamander-covered shield, Christ and the Virgin Mary. The Knights-Templar (*Templiers*), militant Christians whose role was to clear the roads of brigands and protect pilgrims, set up a large headquarters in the village in 1275. Today, old *lauze*-covered houses huddle around this manor house with its tower and fortified gateway.

Slightly west lies **Castel Merle**, another village of *abris* (shelters), nine of which (Abri Labuttat, Abri La Souquette, Abri Reverdit, etc.) were occupied between 30,000 and 10,000 BC and can still be visited. Much of interest was excavated or discovered here, paintings, objects, engravings and artefacts, some of which are on view in the little **Musée Castanet** above the site.

LA FORÊT BARADE

Television salvaged from oblivion a work that should have been a masterpiece in its own right. The spirit of Jacquou le Croquant haunts the Forêt Barade, a thickly wooded area (*barade* in patois means 'closed') to the west of Les Eyzies.

A tall 17th-century stone cross in the centre of the little village of 147 inhabitants, a coping well, a dovecote and a fortified church partially restored in 1706 – **Fanlac** is everything a Périgord village should be. Piles of stones for wall repairs and *lauzes* sit waiting to be used, the village activities continue as though nothing had changed since Jacquou's days. And yet... it's perhaps just a little too manicured to be totally real. Le Roy set the early part of his story here. It's well worth a visit for its site, charm, church and history.

Even if you haven't read *Jacquou le Croquant*, you shouldn't miss the haunting ruins of the **Château de l'Herm**. In the novel, Jacquou **41** sets fire to it; in reality, it simply fell to ruin. Yet its site, beside the humble, derelict hamlet of l'Herm, with its famous twin chimneys rising above the tree line, capture the imagination. Abandoned in 1862 in a pitiful state, Eugène Le Roy gave it, unwittingly, a new lease of life.

Children adore Rouffignac's caves. Here in a 'toy' electric train we penetrate 2 km (1.25 miles) deep into the bowels of the earth to see the **Grotte des Cent Mammouths** (Cave of a Hundred Mammoths). As the engine chugs deeper into the wide gallery, suddenly the guide switches on a lamp to illuminate the most extraordinary scene. For these drawings of mammoth (and other animals such as the hairy rhinoceros, bison, the horse and ibex) are exceptionally easy to distinguish on the wide walls and roof and are in an excellent state of preservation. Note in particular *the Patriarch*, the most imposing of the mammoths. The tusks were carved with a harder instrument than the hair created with a 'chisel'.

Groups of claw marks on the walls reveal the presence of countless generations of bears.

The existence of the cave had been known for centuries. Graffiti had been scribbled all over some drawings, which were only authenticated in 1956 as dating from around 11,000 BC. No stalactites or mineral formations have ever existed although the rock's forms are often decorative, with domes and cupola-like ceilings formed by the pressure of water millions of years ago.

Rouffignac town, 5 km (3 miles) away, looks superficially much like many others in the Dordogne, but on closer inspection it's a new town; the old one was burned down by the Nazis as they retreated. Only the 16th-century **Eglise Saint-Germain** was mercifully spared.

Y*ou'll find truth and fiction, usually far apart in reality, intermingle at the ruins of the Château de l'Herm.*

interest. Particularly well exposed here are the various geological strata that help us understand the changes our planet underwent through the ages.

From a platform about half way up the chasm, you gaze in wonder at the yellow and white concretions that adorn the ceiling of the 'dome' of the **Gouffre de Proumeyssac**. The 300-m (984-ft) tunnel was drilled artificially to facilitate access but the rest is totally natural; as water seeps in, it creates natural formations of stalactites and stalagmites of such beauty that a son-et-lumière show is organized to exploit its possibilities to the full.

Saint-Cyprien's top-heavy abbey crowning the town is renowned for its organ concerts. The town, on a lovely stretch of the Dordogne, is a perfect point of departure to visit the neighbouring attractions.

SAINTS AND *CINGLES*

None of the small localities we visit now is far from either Sarlat or Les Eyzies, in the very heart of the Périgord Noir. But this is a different Dordogne, where caves are less prominent but saints much in evidence.

The engravings of the **Grotte de Bara-Bahau** are somewhat difficult for the layman to decipher, but the bears, ibex, bison and horses, drawn with sharpened flints, dating from the Upper Périgordian or **44** Aurignacian period, are of great

Five km (3 miles) from Le Bugue, the gentle Vézère meets up with the Dordogne, which has been growing steadily more powerful and now makes one of its loops (*cingles*), called the Cingle de Limeuil. At this strategic point, where traffic could be controlled and taxes levied, one of the most beautiful of all Dordogne's villages was built. **Limeuil** has an upper town, set on a spur, and a port below.

The Dordogne takes another horse-shoe meander and coils back on itself, ensnaring **Trémolat**, an enchanting village containing a massive fortress-like 12th-century Romanesque church with a big bell tower.

*M*ontignac has delightful walks along the Vézère and good food, besides being an excellent starting point for visits to Lascaux.

The little abbey-village of **Cadouin** was deliberately sheltered deep in the heart of the Bessède Forest. Robert d'Abrissel, its soldier-founder-monk went there to seek communion with God, not his fellow man. The Cistercian abbey built in 1115 was in the austere tradition of the Order, but it was very prosperous in the Middle Ages, simply because the abbey had obtained the Holy Shroud, the cloth Christ supposedly bore round his head, brought back from the Crusades by a Périgord priest. Pilgrims on their way to Santiago de Compostela made the detour, including no lesser

The river provided a means of transport and stitched the Dordogne together. Castles along it defended the different 'sides' during battles.

figures than Richard the Lion-Heart and St. Louis.

With time and prosperity, the Order's austerity gave way to a certain laxism. The cloister, instead of pure lines and calm surfaces, was decorated with a profusion of the most extraordinary sculpture: scenes and details on the columns, over the doors and on the keystones were anything but severe (Samson and Delilah, Noah's Arc, but also fables and satirical scenes, reminiscent of the paintings of Bosch). Worse was to come: the annual pilgrimage, when the Shroud was borne through Cadouin's streets amid throngs of pilgrims, came to an abrupt end: scholars poring over the Shroud deciphered the embroidered bands of Kufic script, which sung the praises of... Allah. The pilgrimage was discontinued in 1934.

Owing to the Abbey's fame and importance as a pilgrimage centre, it was well restored in the 19th century. The 1154 **church** has the stern, defensive façade of Périgord churches, lightened by a graceful triple-arched doorway with a row of blind arching. Inside, we find the pure lines and austerity of normal Cistercian architecture with three beautiful barrel-vaulted arches. Outside, the village is most picturesque with its small *halles*.

The 12th-century **Saint-Avit-Sénieur** honours yet another soldier-hermit. On the route to Compostela, more fortress than church, Saint-Avit's vast expanses of yellow wall somehow belie its warlike appearance: the crenellations, the tall, virtually blind façade and the twin towers. The forlorn ruins of the cloister lie beside the church.

VILLAGE LIFE

While monasteries and fortress-churches were flourishing, village life was following its eternal rhythm. No part of France, perhaps, has so many villages, manors, châteaux or landscapes of unchanging charm, where even modern villas do not detract from the serenity and boundless feeling of well-being. **47**

From Les Eyzies, Montignac or Sarlat, a short excursion into the hills leads past **Cap Blanc** (some of the finest prehistoric drawings of horses, a monumental frieze along 14 m/46 ft of wall) to **Marquay** and **Tamniès**, very much villages for those that prefer quiet spots to hustle and bustle. Both are well equipped with hotels and are simply charming. A few kilometres on, the stunning ruins of the **Château de Commarque** come into view – ruins, maybe, but haunting, overgrown and romantic, with a long history of violence. After a couple of centuries as a den of armed brigands, it joined the 'wrong' (Huguenot) camp, so Charles IX ordered its destruction in 1569.

The small 15th-century **Château de Laussel** nearby, suspended high on a cliff above the River Beune, has been much restored, but it corresponds to what we expect of a medieval château. However, it derives its fame from the astonishing prehistoric finds made a few hundred yards away. From the deposit, ten levels were excavated, ranging from the Mousterian of 100,000 years ago to Solutrean of 17,000 BC, including the 'primitive' but important statuette of the *Vénus de Laussel*.

On a steep, thickly forested hill, 6 km (4 miles) out of Sarlat, emerges the elegant silhouette of the **Château de Puymartin**. While it is classical outside, built in yellow limestone and roofed with *lauzes*, it is really the exceptional decoration inside that makes a visit so interesting. The château has been in the same family for 500 years, giving it a particular unity.

Crossing to the other side of the Sarlat to the Montignac road, **Saint-Geniès** is the perfect example of a Périgord Noir village, a showpiece, but all perfectly genuine. The church, manor house and cosy dwellings, uniformly roofed in *lauzes,* glow in the sunshine amid a profusion of vegetation. Nothing prepares you for the **Chapelle du Cheylard** with its minute chapel harbouring some of the freshest frescoes imaginable (1327-29); some of

*S*t. Geniès is the type of village which gives the Dordogne its reputation. Every house, with its lauze roof, harmonizes with the whole. **49**

St. Amand-de-Coly, certainly one of the most impressive of the Périgord's fortified churches, also has music festivals and craftsmen like this metal worker (dimandier).

the cruellest, too, as Catherine is tortured and souls are precipitated down to fry in hell.

Château de Salignac-Eyvigues lies on a rock which stands well out from the hillside and the village. Built in various stages between the 12th and 17th centuries, the château has kept its ramparts and some mullioned windows on the main building, flanked by two round towers capped by pepper pots. The village beside it has a honey-coloured covered market and delightful

Renaissance houses in old alleyways. If you enjoy gardens, the Dordogne's best example is at **Eyrignac** – the château is 17th-18th century and the **gardens** are very much *à la française* and trimmed to a tee.

If you had to choose just one church to visit in the whole of the Dordogne, it should be **Saint-Amand-de-Coly**: the majestic fortified abbey-church overwhelms the little village beneath it. Size in churches usually meant importance: from early days, Saint-Amand had a large defensive role to play with ramparts, a parapet walk, turrets and a former drawbridge, not to mention the portal-cum-dungeon. If its true origins go back to the 7th century, the driving force behind its construction came from the Augustinian Abbé Guillaume,

'a noble man' as it states on his tombstone, some time between 1124–30. However, the Abbey went into decline in the following centuries, finding itself with only seven monks in 1347 and two in 1430.

The massively tall recessed portal, the excessively pure lines, the relatively little decoration and sculpture immediately strike you. Even inside, where the floor slopes quite sharply upwards, the defensive appearance is omnipresent: slit windows, stairways hidden in pillars, the apse lit only by three bays and a bull's-eye window, as well as three defensive positions at ground level near the chancel. The architect, a military genius with spiritual leanings, took into account successive lines of defence if one or the other collapsed. And yet, paradoxically, Saint-Amand-de-Coly is to many visitors the church in the Périgord whose spirituality is the most tangible and moving. Little wonder it is often used for concert festivals. **51**

Périgord Blanc

Périgord Blanc (white because of the limestone) covers the central stretch of the province, taking in Périgueux, the capital. Most of the way it is accompanied by the quiet River Isle, or in the east, the boisterous Auvézère so appreciated by anglers and canoe enthusiasts. If we lose some of the 'drama' of the Périgord Noir, we enter an area of gentle green hills and vales, walnut-growing in the eastern parts in the Pays d'Ans, strawberries in the south round Vergt, small forgotten hamlets and communities, charming in their own right but with fewer major monuments.

PÉRIGUEUX

Yes, you should visit Périgueux despite what you may have heard.

The different layers of the city provide a fascinating panorama of 20 centuries if you choose your day (for local colour, Wednesday, market day); refuse to depart from your habitual calm because of traffic problems and don't shrink before a little grime in some of the medieval areas. The city is in two parts: la Cité, grouped around the Roman town, and the Puy Saint-Front, under the shadow of the domes of the cathedral. Half a day's visit gives you a good impression of both.

Slowly but surely, the capital of the Dordogne is sprucing itself up and in a few years will be a real showplace. First point in its favour: Périgueux provides the best ensemble of Roman remains in the Périgord. The Gallo-Roman circuit lies half a mile outside the city centre. Barely enough of the

*P*érigueux's cathedral, unfortunately restored in the last century, is best appreciated at night or reflected in the River Isle below.

arena, now a garden, remains to suggest the 20,000 spectators howling for blood during the gory spectacles.

The colossal **Tour de Vésone**, a round 30-m (98-ft) high, 20-m (66-ft) diameter tower, once the sacred core of the *cella,* was probably part of a huge temple complex dedicated to the titular goddess of the city.

The Renaissance and medieval parts of the town centre, the Puy Saint-Front quarter, are mostly pedestrian-only (interesting walking tours are arranged by the Tourist Office). However, strolling around the exceptionally lively markets is best done alone: place du Coderc and place de l'Hôtel de Ville in the shadow of the cathedral are best for fruit and vegetables, place de la Clautre for poultry and everything else on Wednesdays and Saturdays, place Saint-Louis in winter for *foie gras* and truffles.

The **Cathédral Saint-Front** remains a subject of controversy. It is one of the biggest cathedrals in southern France and, left alone, would have **53** been an unrivalled example of Périgord Romanesque. Unfortunately, the well-intentioned 19th-century restorer Abadie felt he could 'improve' it. Fortunately, he left the 12th-century bell tower as it was, but the rest he rebuilt to the taste of the day. The 12th–16th-century cloister remains a haven of peace beside the busy market, but it is from outside that the cathedral is best appreciated. Its array of pine-cone-covered pinnacles and bulbous white cupolas towering over the houses around, the whole reflected in the river, make a charming tableau seen from the Pont des Barris bridge below.

OUT AND ABOUT IN PÉRIGORD BLANC

A few miles out of Périgueux, the Augustinian abbey of **Chancelade** was founded in 1129 by a hermit, Foucault, with the benediction and protection of the Bishops of Périgueux. This support in high places came in useful, for the **54** abbey found itself bestowed with numerous privileges and influence – and wealth. Whence a sizeable abbey church with some graceful Romanesque features and later alterations that do nothing to detract from the pure harmony of the whole.

To the north lies **Saint-Astier** and the vast, mysterious Forêt de la Double. The town itself is an excellent departure point for exploring the weird and wonderful world of maritime pine wood and pond, extending almost up to agricultural **Ribérac**, where cereal farming and cattle raising begin again. At **Siorac-de-Ribérac**, the *cluzeaux* (lookout caves), so often seen near the Vézère, reappear – but by this time we are in the Périgord Vert. If we allow ourselves one rapid incursion over to the Charente *département* next door, it should be to Aubeterre's fascinating monolithic church cut out of the rock, originally built in the 6th century and completed in the Middle Ages.

When approached from behind, the **Château des Bories** retains a faintly feudal aspect, with its moat and massive square tower, but from the front it has all the graces we expect of a Renaissance château: flat open forecourt, the River Isle streaming by and inside a staircase of majestic proportions. The *galerie*, a great hall with a superb wooden ceiling, boasts two fireplaces, one big enough to roast an ox, the other a Renaisssance jewel with the family arms. Started in 1497, the château took the Saint-Astier family about a century to build, by which time tastes were very much more suave.

The **Château de Hautefort** is a pure Renaissance masterpiece. It is so imposing that it dominates the hill and village at its feet. Its elegance and symmetry, trimmed hedges and gardens *à la française* impress every visitor.

Searching for Truffles

The Romans had known them, and even Mme. de Pompadour believed in their aphrodisiac virtues and ate them whenever she could 'to keep the love of Louis XV'. Yet today, truffles still remain a mystery. Why do they only grow under certain trees? How are they detected? Does it really need a pig with a *caveur* (truffle-finder) to sniff out their presence? The Ecomusée de la Truffe in **Sorges**, capital of the truffle area, goes a long way in clearing up these mysteries concerning the 'black diamond' of Périgord cuisine, with the aid of maps, panels, films and photos. In the 1870s they were an appreciated rarity but 6,000 tons were harvested; today, a mere 9 tons find their way onto the market. If the museum can't actually give you a taste, it sends you off on a two-hour hike through an area of *truffières* (truffle beds) where they *have* been known to be found.

55

The last vestiges of feudal times, the barbican with the two lookout towers on either side, the drawbridge and 'half-moat' from 1588 give out over the vast gravel forecourt. Inside, two round towers capped **56** with domes and lantern turrets hem in the inner court, with the main body of the building on three sides. The harmonious slate-covered roof adds to the perfection of the overall impression.

The main builder would appear to have been Jacques-

ruined it. The owners, with the help of the Ministry, are painstakingly restoring and redecorating it.

The tumultuous River Auvézère tumbles down from the hills of Corrèze. By the time it reaches sleepy **Tourtoirac**, it eases gracefully past the green banks, a popular summer recreation and picnic spot, and bathes the gardens of the former **abbey**. In the 13th century, the prosperous Benedictine abbey had 35 monks, but declined during the Wars of Religion and, after a 'visit' by the Huguenots, was more or less abandoned. Of the Romanesque church, only the transept and towers, one square (reminiscent of Saint-Amand-de-Coly), the other pointed, remain.

François de Hautefort, around 1630 (the building took 40 years), whom Molière used as the model for his miser, Harpagon, in *L'Avare*.

A cigarette stub negligently abandoned in August 1968 set fire to the château and all but

Périgord Vert

The Périgord Vert and Blanc merge imperceptibly into one another. The Périgord Vert is what it says – a green crescent taking in the north of the province, where the lakes, streams and ponds converge towards the rivers Dronne, Isle, Côle and Auvézère, keeping the area cool even in the height of summer. It offers many of the same pleasures as the Périgord Noir and other 'colours' but it does have a plus – some of the finest châteaux.

BRANTÔME COUNTRY

No, it's not another Venice as it is sometimes called – even if it gives the impression of being on an island. **Brantôme** simply dreams on within its loop in the River Dronne. The reflections of the gardens and houses in the serene waters, the white stone of the abbey huddling beneath the limestone cliffs and the troglodyte caves behind set a romantic scene. The elegant Renaissance pavilion (now the Tourist Office), with its mullioned windows beside the right-angled, 'L'-shaped bridge (*pont coudé*) crossing to the formal 'Monk's Garden', add a final touch of charm. Over it all floats the presence of Pierre de Bourdeille, called Brantôme, a Benedictine abbot, but very much an adventurer and a *galant homme*, as well as a distinguished author.

In 786 Charlemagne gave to the newly constructed monastery the relics for a shrine to St. Sicaire. After devastating Viking raids in the 10th century, it was reconstructed, developing under French and English sovereignty until Bourdeille was appointed abbot in 1557. He only actually settled there when a bad fall from a horse in 1583 gave him no choice but to devote his time to writing, which he did in the little Renaissance lodge. This swashbuckling warrior turned Brantôme into

From the Bourdeilles château tower, the view is magnificent. The furniture inside is superb.

Uniting the useful and the pleasant. At Périgueux's famous market, a good gossip can combine with shopping suggestions.

the most wealthy, flourishing monastery in Aquitaine, but after his death in 1614 all went to rack and ruin. The 19th-century restorer Claude Abadie arrived and 'saved' the church by transforming it to the taste of the day. Fortunately he left the 11th-century Charlemagne tower as it was: it remains the oldest bell tower in France.

You should look in at the **church** to admire its proportions, not totally ruined despite Abadie's heavy-handed restoration work. The one original Romanesque column salvaged from the old church, now used as a font, depicts the Massacre of the Innocents.

The **abbey** is interesting for its monumental classical stairway and its monks' dormitory with remarkable timberwork. More poignant, however, is a visit to the **caves** behind the building, which the monks used as a bakery and wine cellar. Little is known about the 14th–15th-century **sculptures** carved directly into the rock, but they form an absolutely magical setting for an annual classical dance spectacle. In summer, there are also concerts of a high order.

The **Château de Bourdeilles** is really two châteaux in one: a medieval fortress with a Renaissance manor house within its walls. Entry is through no less than three curtain walls – a tell-tale indication that this was a fought-over château.

When Louis XI handed over the existing barony to the English in 1259, one of the four most important in the Périgord, he split the Bourdeille family: one half joined the English Plantagenets, the other, the Maumonts, simply refused. Thus, the château changed hands, with the Maumonts taking it for a time and fortifying it as it lay in the heart of an English-occupied part of the country.

HISTORY AND PREHISTORY

Three sights of particular interest are grouped around the village of Villars: the cave of Villars, the château of Puyguilhem and the ruins of Boschaud Abbey.

The **Château de Puyguilhem** is often considered the most complete Renaissance château in the Dordogne: gone are all warlike features, everything here is geared to the senses. From the approach down a long tree-lined drive to the magnificent façade all is grace, calm and harmony.

Inside, admire the mantelpiece on the first floor, with its shell-shaped niches of sculptures depicting six of the twelve labours of Hercules, and the formidable staircase that has a coffered ceiling with hanging keystones. On the second floor, the chestnut timberwork roofing in the form of an upturned vessel displays the skill of rafters, many of whom were apprentice shipbuilders.

Although the vast majority of prehistoric finds have been **61**

It doesn't lead into the dungeon: it's the way up to the roof of the Bourdeilles château's tower.

along or near the Vézère, there was no doubt as much going on in the caves, shelters and hideaways of the Isle. Excavations are producing interesting finds but the most important discovered so far is the **Grotte de Villars**, deep in the heart of a wood. Not only do you see some magnificent stalactites, astonishingly pure white concretions and a multitude of fascinating, almost lunar rock formations, but you also find the famous *Blue Horse* (covered in a fine film of calcite, which imparts this particular blue hue) among some 30 drawings going back to at least 17,000 BC.

Saint-Jean-de-Côle is what one always imagined a village to be like in times past. At the far end of the gravel and earth square, a covered market cuddles up against a tall church; down one side runs a row of snug houses bordered by flowers and shrubs; facing them, a small château and a couple of rival inns back-to-back. At the bottom of the village, a cobblestone Gothic humpback bridge leapfrogs over the tiny River Côle (a tributary of the Dronne),

with a mill to one side, a manor on the other and an islet in the middle.

Although not much remains of the original 12th-century **Château de la Marthonie**, it adds a harmonious element to the village square. The Huguenots pillaged it in 1569; the towers remain from those troubled times, but the graceful arcaded part was constructed in the 17th century.

Pay your respects to *foie gras* by visiting the interesting museum devoted to it at the market town of **Thiviers**, in a little room beside the *Syndicat* **63**

*B*rantôme Abbey reflected in the dreamy waters of the Dronne.

set about 'modernizing' the existing fortress-château, creating something most romantic, decorative and totally unconventional – but not terribly habitable.

The village around the vast esplanade, that used to hold the pig fair, slopes down to the proud château parapet, while pepper-pot turrets, dormer windows and chimneys encircle the so-called *chapeau du marquis* (Marquis' Hat), a round belvedere lookout turret. The leaden finials are particularly imaginative in their designs from angels to birds. Inside is less interesting than out but like all good châteaux, a legend surrounds the portrait of Louise de Hautefort, called *La Fileuse* (The Spinner): locked away for twenty years by a jealous husband, she sent messages via a spindle to her lover who became a shepherd on the farm in order to stay beside her.

d'Initiative (Tourist Office). Thiviers is the 'capital' of *foie gras*, and to get to know a real Périgord market, there's none better.

Jumilhac-le-Grand guards the north-eastern border of the Périgord Vert, and it could scarcely find a better representative to do so. If it is not exactly a 'rags to riches' story, it is true that a local farmer-cum-blacksmith who had made good after marrying a wealthy heiress was ennobled in 1597 for helping to finance the future Henri IV's campaigns. He

A Selection of Dordogne Hotels and Restaurants

Recommended Hotels and Restaurants

The range of hotels in the Dordogne runs the gamut of expensive – but not excessively so – to very reasonable. In our list we make two categories: luxury and the medium-to-economic. There are plenty of 'lower bracket' options, 'bed-and-breakfasts' and small one- or no-star hotels are becoming more and more popular, but these are constantly changing, so it is safer to check on the spot with local tourist offices to avoid disappointment. Most – but not all – of the establishments mentioned are hotels and restaurants, which binds you (only morally) to eat where you sleep. We have categorized our listing by locality and have provided the postal code with the name of the village in case you wish to book in advance.

Our criterion for Luxury Hotels and Restaurants has been: 400–900 F half board (room, evening meal plus breakfast, per person); for Medium and Family-Run Hotels and Restaurants: 250–400 F half board (room, evening meal plus breakfast, per person).

Luxury Hotels and Restaurants

ANTONNE-ET-TRIGONANT 24220
Hôtel-Restaurant des Chandelles. Tel. 53 06 05 10 11 km (7 miles) from Périgueux. Charming 15th-century residence in a park, with a swimming pool and tennis courts. Classical cuisine (fish specialities). 7 rooms. Closed mid-Jan. to mid-Feb and Mon out of season.

BERGERAC–ST. JULIEN-DE-CREMPSE 24140

Manoir le Grand Vignoble.
Tel. 53 24 23 18
12 km (7.5 miles) from Bergerac by the N21 and D107. Louis XIV manor house surrounded by a sizeable park. Swimming pool, tennis courts, sauna. Gourmet cuisine. 38 rooms. Closed 23 Dec to 13 Jan.

BIRAS-BOURDEILLES 24310

Château de la Côte.
Tel. 53 03 70 11
3 km (2 miles) from Bourdeilles, 10 km (6 miles) from Brantôme. 18th-century château in the middle of a magnificent park. Swimming pool, horse-riding. Excellent cuisine. 14 high-class rooms and suites. Open all year round.

BOURDEILLES 24310

Hotellerie Les Griffons.
Tel. 53 03 75 61
16th-century house on the River Dronne. Lovely dining room. Regional cuisine. 10 extremely comfortable rooms. Closed from 15 Oct to Palm Sunday.

BRANTÔME 24310

Moulin de l'Abbaye.
Tel. 53 05 80 22
Dream-like mill on the River Dronne. The dining room has a terrace overlooking the river. Regional specialities. 9 luxurious rooms and 3 apartments. Closed from 25 Oct to 4 May.

Hôtel-Restaurant Chabrol.
Tel. 53 05 70 15
Establishment with a very high reputation in a town house beside the River Dronne, virtually facing the abbey. Regional specialities beautifully prepared. 19 rooms. Closed 15 Nov to 15 Dec and 5 to 23 Feb.

Moulin du Roc at Champagnac de Belair. Tel. 53 54 80 36
6 km (4 miles) north east of Brantôme. Former oil-mill that has kept its machinery and its charm. Local and regional specialities. 10 rooms and 4 apartments. Closed from 15 Nov to 15 Dec and from 15 Jan to 15 Feb.

67

BUGUE, LE 24260

Hôtel-Restaurant Royal-Vézère. Tel. 53 07 20 01
Grand palace beside the Vézère right in the centre of Le Bugue. Panoramic terrace with a swimming pool on the roof. Sumptuous interior. 49 rooms and 4 suites. The Albuca, its restaurant, enjoys an excellent reputation. Closed 1 Oct to 30 Apr.

LE BUISSON DE CADOUIN 24480

Le Manoir de Bellerive.
Tel. 53 27 16 19
Manor house beside the Dordogne. In a park with a swimming pool and tennis courts. 16 rooms. There is no restaurant but you can enjoy an excellent buffet breakfast. Closed 1 Nov. to 15 Apr.

COLY-TERRASSON 24120

Manoir de Hautegente.
Tel. 53 51 68 03
Ivy-covered manor house right in the heart of the Périgord Noir. Antique furniture. Refined cuisine. 10 rooms. English spoken. Closed from 11 Nov to 1 Apr.

CONDAT-SUR-VÉZÈRE 24570

Château de la Fleunie.
Tel. 53 51 32 74
5 km (3 miles) from Lascaux on a large estate, this château guarantees comfort and tranquillity. Swimming pool, tennis court, golf, horse-riding. Gourmet cuisine. 22 rooms. Closed in Jan.

DOMME 24250

Hôtel-Restaurant l'Esplanade.
Tel. 53 28 31 41
Lovely Périgord house on the Belvédère de la Barre, at the top of the town with a fabulous view of the Dordogne valley. Reasonably priced regional specialities. 19 period-style rooms. Closed 15 Nov to 15 Feb.

LES EYZIES-DE-TAYAC 24620

Hôtel-Restaurant Le Cente-naire. Tel. 53 06 97 18
Right in the centre of the charming village, in a Périgord-style house, this is a much respected establishment. Garden with swimming pool, gym. Refined interior decoration. Périgord specialities in line with today's tastes. 20 sumptuous rooms and 4 apartments. Closed 1 Nov to 1 Apr.

Hôtel-Restaurant Cro-magnon. Tel. 53 06 97 06
Located beside the Cro-magnon deposit and near the church of Tayac, this is a beautiful ivy-covered house, surrounded by a flower garden with a swimming pool. Exhibition of archaeological objects. Very good Périgord cuisine. 20 rooms and 4 apartments. Closed 13 Oct to the end of Apr.

Moulin de la Beune. Tel. 53 06 94 33
Former mill on the River Beune. Rustic décor. Very refined cuisine. 20 charming rooms. Closed Nov to Mar.

MONPAZIER 24540

Hôtel Edward Ier. Tel. 53 22 44 00
19th-century town house right inside the *bastide* but in a quiet street, surrounded by a garden with a swimming pool. 13 personalized rooms. No restaurant. Closed 15 Nov to Easter.

MONTIGNAC 24290

Château de Puy Robert. Tel. 53 51 92 13
1.5 km (1 mile) south west of Montignac. Deep in the heart of a pleasant park with a swimming pool, this hotel-restaurant is housed in an adorable Napoleon III château. Elegant interior decoration. Refined gourmet cuisine. 33 luxury rooms and 5 apartmernts. Closed from 15 Oct to 1 May.

Le Relais du Soleil d'Or. Tel. 53 51 80 22
A former mail-coach inn in a small park with a swimming pool. Périgord specialities adapted to today's tastes. 28 rooms and 4 apartments. Closed 15 Jan to 15 Feb.

MONTPON-MÉNESTÉROL 24700

Château des Grillauds.
Tel. 53 80 49 71
18th-century château surrounded by greenery, with a swimming pool and tennis courts. Refined and innovative cuisine. Very elegant dining room. (Restaurant closed Sunday evening). 7 rooms. Closed in Jan.

RAZAC-SUR-L'ISLE 24430

Château de Lalande.
Tel. 53 54 52 30
12 km (7.5 miles) from Périgueux, this château-hotel is magnificently located. Local cuisine. Tranquil setting in a park with a swimming pool. 22 rooms. Closed from 15 Nov to 15 Mar.

SAINT-CYPRIEN 24220

Hôtel-Restaurant l'Abbaye.
Tel. 53 29 20 48
An old house at the top of a hill. Garden at the back with a swimming pool. Meals served out on the terrace. 24 rooms. Closed 15 Oct to 10 Apr.

SAINT GENIÈS 24590

Hôtel-Restaurant La Peyrière.
Tel. 53 28 98 12
Right in the heart of Périgord Noir, surrounded by greenery in a 6- hectare (15-acre) park. 12 apartments each with 2 bedrooms, living-room with kitchenette, bathroom and terrace. Golf course attached. Excellent Périgord cuisine and warm welcome.

SARLAT 24200

La Couleuvrine.
Tel. 53 59 27 80
Historic old house nestling in the old ramparts. Fresh inventive cuisine with local produce and specialities. 26 rooms. Closed 10 to 31 Jan and 15 to 30 Nov.

Hôtel-Restaurant La Madeleine. Tel. 53 59 10 41
Large comfortable house very near medieval Sarlat. There is an elegant dining room. Cuisine highlighting Sarlat specialities. 19 rooms and 3 apartments. Closed 11 Nov to 15 Mar.

Hostellerie de Meysset.
Tel. 53 59 08 29
Ivy-covered Périgord house in the countryside 2 km (1.25 miles) from Sarlat on the Les Eyzies road. Meals served on the terrace overlooking the whole valley. Regional specialities. 22 very quiet rooms and 4 apartments. Closed 13 Oct to 20 Apr.

SAVIGNAC-LES-EGLISES 24420

Hôtel-Restaurant le Parc.
Tel. 53 05 07 60
Former mail-coach inn in a pleasant park. Gym and health club. Creative modern cuisine respecting Périgord traditions. Hotel school with high reputation. 11 personalized rooms. Closed from 1 Oct to 15 May.

THIVIERS 24800

Château-Hôtel de Mauraleix.
Tel. 53 52 82 01
16th-century château ideal for conventions. The park, with a swimming pool, is particularly good for riding. Local cuisine. Restaurant closed Wed. 22 dream-like rooms. Closed 3 Jan to 7 Feb.

TRÉMOLAT 24510

Le Vieux Logis.
Tel. 53 22 80 66
A Périgord mansion surrounded by delightful trimmed gardens, with a swimming pool. Beautiful interior décor with period furniture and an elegant dining room. High-quality Périgord cuisine with local specialities. 14 rooms and 8 apartments. Closed 7 Jan to 18 Feb.

VIEUX-MAREUIL 24340

Château du Vieux-Mareuil.
Tel. 53 60 77 15
15th-century house in a large park, with a pool overlooking the valley. Imaginative but traditional-style cuisine. 14 rooms. Closed 15 Jan to 28 Feb.

Medium and Family-Run Hotels and Restaurants

BADEFOLS-D'ANS 24390

Hôtel-Restaurant Les Tilleuls. Tel. 53 51 52 97
Pleasant, quiet hotel off the beaten track. 7 rooms.

BEAUMONT 24440

Hôtel-Restaurant Les Voyageurs. Tel. 53 22 30 11
Very comfortable village hotel, particularly well run and very popular. The restaurant gives exceptional value for money. 10 rooms. Closed mid-Oct to mid-Nov, Jan, Feb and Mon except in July/Aug.

BELVES 24170

Hôtel-Restaurant Le Home. Tel. 53 29 01 65
Hotel with shaded terrace. Traditional cuisine. 10 rooms. Open every day except for 10 days in March.

BERGERAC 24100

Europ Hôtel. Tel. 53 57 06 54
Quiet hotel with a swimming pool. No restaurant. 22 rooms.

Hôtel-Restaurant de Bordeaux. Tel. 53 57 12 83
Lovely house in a park with a swimming pool. 41 rooms. Closed 20 Dec to 30 Jan.

Hôtel-Restaurant La Flambée. Tel. 53 57 52 33
Pleasant buildings in a park with a swimming pool. Regional cuisine. 21 rooms.

BEYNAC 24220

Hôtel-Restaurant du Château. Tel. 53 29 50 13
Superb house beside the Dordogne. Regional cuisine. 21 very comfortable rooms. Closed 1 Jan to 10 Mar.

Hotel-Restaurant Bonnet. Tel. 53 29 50 01
Périgord house in a garden beside the Dordogne. Regional specialities. 22 rooms with a view over the river and garden. Closed 15 Oct to 18 Apr.

Hotel-Restaurant Pontet-Male-ville. Tel. 53 29 50 06
Traditional Périgord house offering a warm welcome. Périgord specialities. 16 rooms. Closed for a fortnight in Nov and a fortnight in Feb.

BOUNIAGUES 24560

Hôtel-Restaurant des Voyageurs. Tel. 53 58 32 26
In the middle of the Bergerac vineyards but beside a main road (RN21). Meals served in the garden behind. Local cuisine. 9 rooms. Closed 15 Oct to 15 Nov and Sun and Mon evenings.

BRANTÔME 24310

Auberge du Soir.
Tel. 53 05 82 93
16th-century inn, centrally located. 8 comfortable rooms. Closed 15 Jan to 15 Feb.

Fermand'el. Tel. 53 05 70 58
Pretty house at the bottom of a garden, very calm, just outside the town centre. 16 rooms. Closed Sun evening and Fri from 11 Nov to 28 Feb.

BUGUE, LE 24260

Hôtel de Paris.
Tel. 53 07 28 16
Very simple but agreeable village hotel. Shady terrace. 22 rooms. Open all year.

Hôtel-Restaurant du Château at Campagn. Tel. 53 07 23 50
House in a garden facing the château. 6 km (4 miles) from Les Eyzies. Ideal for exploring the Périgord Noir. Traditional cuisine. 18 very comfortable rooms. Closed from 15 Oct to 24 Mar.

CADOUIN

Auberge de la Salvétat.
Tel. 53 22 92 08
Housed in a 12th-century farmhouse on the edge of the forest of Bessède. Swimming pool. Rustic dining room. Renowned for its cuisine. 8 rooms. Closed from 11 Nov to 1 May.

CARSAC-AILLAC 24200

Hôtel-Restaurant Delpeyrat.
Tel. 53 28 10 43
Small but well-kept hotel 19 km (12 miles) from Sarlat. 14 **73**

rooms. Closed from 10 Oct to 10 Nov and from 10 to 28 Feb.

Hôtel-Restaurant Le Relais du Touron. Tel. 53 28 16 70
An excellent place to stay. 8 km (5 miles) from Sarlat. The hotel is in a park with a swimming pool and lake. Refined cuisine. 12 cosy rooms. Closed 15 Nov to 15 Mar.

CHANCELADE 24650
Hôtel-Restaurant Du Pont de la Beauronne.
Tel. 53 08 42 91
Périgord house in the Périgord Blanc. 3 km (2 miles) from Périgueux. A family atmosphere. Regional cuisine. 30 rooms. Closed 20 Sept to 20 Oct, Sun evening and Mon morning.

CHERVEIX-CUBAS 24390
Hôtel-Restaurant Chez Favard. Tel. 53 50 41 05
Ask for rooms in the new annex with a view over the countryside and swimming

pool. Busy road in front. *Menus* for hearty appetites. 13 rooms. Closed from 15 to 30 Oct.

DOMME 24250
Hôtel-Restaurant Le Nouvel Hôtel. Tel. 53 28 38 67
Old house in the heart of a beautiful *bastide*. Local cuisine. 17 modern rooms. Closed Jan and Feb.

DOUVILLE 24140
Hôtel-Restaurant Tropicana. Tel. 53 82 98 31
Next to a 2-hectare (5-acre) lake with boats, pedaloes, water-toboggans for hire, plus many other activities. All are included in the price of your stay. Swimming pool. Garden. 23 rooms. Good food. Closed 20 Dec to 17 Feb.

EXCIDEUIL 24160
Hôtel-Restaurant du Fin Chapon. Tel. 53 62 42 38
A house with a shady terrace below the château. Regional cuisine. 10 rooms. Closed 15 De. to 15 Jan.

LES EYZIES-DE-TAYAC 24620

Hôtel-Restaurant du Centre.
Tel. 53 06 97 13
Lovely old house in the centre of town. Meals served on the terrace. 20 rooms. Closed from 15 Nov to 15 Mar.

Hôtel des Roches.
Tel. 53 06 96 59
Converted old farmhouse in a sizeable garden with the River Beune behind. Swimming pool. 28 very comfortable rooms. Closed from Nov to Apr.

FLEURAC 24580

Hôtel-Restaurant La Coste Jaubert. Tel. 53 05 49 19
Tranquil, verdant setting next to a brook. Close to several châteaux and other sights. Swimming pool. Family atmosphere. 5 comfortable rooms. Gourmet and homely cuisine. Open all year round.

LA FORCE 24130

Hostellerie Des Ducs.
Tel. 53 58 95 63
9 km (5.5 miles) from Berge-rac, a small hotel with refined cuisine. 12 rooms. Closed from 1 to 15 Oct and Feb.

GÉNIS 24160

Hôtel-Restaurant Le Relais St. Pierre. Tel. 53 52 47 11
Small village hotel with very acceptable standards. 7 rooms. Open all year.

GROLÉJAC 24250

Hôtel-Restaurant le Gril-lardin. Tel. 53 28 11 02
House at the bottom of a big garden with a pool. Meals served on the outdoor terrace. 14 rooms. Closed from 1 Nov to 1 Mar.

ISSIGEAC 24560

Hôtel-Restaurant la Brucelière. Tel. 53 58 72 28
A pretty house outside the town centre. Refined cuisine. 9 pleasant rooms. Closed 24 Jun to 1 Jul, from 4 to 27 Nov and 5 to 29 Feb.

LALINDE 24150

Hôtel-Restaurant du Château.
Tel. 53 61 01 82
Little château overhanging the Dordogne. Meals served outside on the terrace. Renowned cuisine. 8 rooms some of which have a view over the river. Closed from 1 Dec to 11 Mar and restaurant closed Fri except in Jul/Aug.

Hôtel-Restaurant La Forge.
Tel. 53 24 92 24
Hotel beside the Dordogne just at the entrance to the small town. Shady terrace. Lovely dining room in a former ironworks. Highly reputed cuisine. Some studios with kitchenettes. 21 extremely comfortable rooms. Closed in Jan.

LE LARDIN 24570

Hôtel-Restaurant Sautet.
Tel. 53 51 27 22
Traditionally known and respected hotel in a flower garden with a swimming pool. Périgord cuisine. 34 rooms. Closed from 20 Dec to 15 Jan, Sat and Sun.

LIMEUIL 24510

Hôtel-Restaurant Les Terrasses de Beauregard.
Tel. 53 22 03 15
Lovely house outside the village, dominating the Dordogne from the Cingle de Limeuil. Very quiet. Excellent cuisine. 8 rooms. Closed from 1 Oct to 1 May.

MARQUAY 24620

Hôtel-Restaurant des Bories.
Tel. 53 29 67 02
Ideal halt in a quiet little village 12 km (7.5 miles) from Sarlat. Garden with swimming pool overlooking the whole of the Périgord Noir. Excellent imaginative cuisine. 28 rooms including 2 apartments for 4 persons. Closed from 15 Nov to 15 Mar.

MOLIERES 24480

Hôtel-Restaurant Gaulhiac.
Tel. 53 22 51 40
Family atmosphere. Excellent farm produce served in the restaurant. 5 comfortable rooms.

Shop selling produce. Nuts, pâté, *foie gras*, *confit de canard* etc. Tours round the farm Tues and Fri in Jul and Aug.

MONPAZIER 24540

Hôtel-Restaurant de France. Tel. 53 22 60 06
Hotel with a long history (Lawrence of Arabia stayed here). Good cuisine. 13 pretty rooms. It is open all year round.

MONTFERRAND DU PÉRIGORD 24440

Hôtel-Restaurant Lou Peyrol. Tel. 53 22 33 63
Very pleasant halt in a charming village off the beaten track. 7 rooms. Closed from 1 Oct to 31 Mar.

MONTIGNAC 24290

Hôtel-Restaurant Le Lascaux. Tel. 53 51 82 81
Family-type hotel with special menus for children. Périgord cuisine. 16 rooms. Closed 15 Nov to 31 Jan.

PÉRIGUEUX 24000

Hôtel Bristol. Tel. 53 08 75 90
Modern hotel right in the centre of town, in a quiet location. 29 rooms. There is no restaurant. Closed 23 Dec to 2 Jan.

Hôtel-Restaurant du Périgord. Tel. 53 53 33 63
Charming hotel at the bottom of a garden. Refined cuisine. 20 rooms. Closed 20 Oct to 3 Nov, Feb school holidays.

Hôtel des Arènes. Tel. 53 53 49 85
Peaceful hotel situated in the Gallo-Roman part of town. 19 rooms. Open all year round.

RIBERAC 24600

Hôtel-Restaurant de France. Tel. 53 90 00 61
The charm of the country at this delightful, warm family hotel. Discover Périgord Vert cuisine at its best. Horse-riding, garden. 20 rooms. Closed 5 Jan to 27 Jan and Fri nights and Sat lunchtime 15 Nov to 28 Feb.

ROQUE-GAGEAC, LA 24250

Hôtel-Restaurant La Gardette. Tel. 53 29 51 58 Périgord-style house beside the Dordogne. Shady terrace. High-standard cuisine. 15 rooms. Closed 15 Oct to 24 Mar.

Hôtel-Restaurant de la Belle Etoile. Tel. 53 29 51 44 Family house in a rustic setting. Shady terrace with a view of the Dordogne. Traditional cuisine. 17 rooms. Closed 15 Oct to 1 Apr.

Hôtel-Restaurant Le Périgord. Tel. 53 28 36 55 Modern house in a park between Sarlat and Domme. Swimming pool on the broad lawn. Imaginative specialities. 40 comfortable rooms (half-board only). Closed from 5 Nov to 20 Mar.

SAINT-AMAND-DE-COLY 24290

Hôtel-Restaurant Gardette. Tel. 53 51 68 50 Pleasant family hotel with terrace. Périgord cuisine. 6 rooms. Closed from 15 Nov to Easter.

SAINT-CYPRIEN 24220

Hôtel-Restaurant de la Terrasse. Tel. 53 29 21 69 Small hotel, with meals served on the terrace in summer. Local dishes. 17 rooms. Closed from 1 Nov to 20 Mar.

SAINT-GENIÈS 24590

Hôtel-Restaurant Le Relais des Touristes. Tel. 53 28 97 60 Family hotel in a dream-like village. Meals served in a shady park. 12 rooms. Closed from 1 Oct to 1 Mar.

SAINT-JEAN-DE-CÔLE 24800

Hôtel-Restaurant Le Saint-Jean. Tel. 53 52 23 20 Small and simple hotel in the heart of the old village. 8 rooms. Open all year round.

SALIGNAC-EYVIGUES 24590

Hôtel-Restaurant La Terrasse. Tel. 53 28 80 38 Modern house. Excellent local cuisine. 14 comfortable rooms. Closed from 15 Oct to 24 Mar.

SARLAT-LA-CANÉDA 24200

Hôtel-Restaurant Chez Marcel. Tel. 53 59 21 98
Just outside the city centre on a busy road, this old-style hotel is excellent value for money. Périgord cuisine. 14 rooms. Closed from 1 Dec to 15 Feb.

SIORAC-EN-PÉRIGORD 24170

Auberge de la Petite Reine. Tel. 53 31 60 42
Hotel club with activities in July and August. Two swimming pools. Tennis courts. Special rates for groups (arranged tours and guide). 39 rooms. Closed from 1 Nov to 15 Apr.

SORGES 24420

Hôtel-Restaurant Auberge de la Truffe. Tel. 53 05 02 05
Park-garden with swimming pool. Meals served on the terrace. Refined Périgord cuisine. Courses in the preparation of *foie gras* in summer. 19 comfortable rooms (but avoid those facing the main road). Hearty buffet breakfast. Hotel open the whole year.

Hôtel-Restaurant de la Mairie. Tel. 53 05 02 11
Small, traditional hotel. Regional cuisine with modern innovations. 8 rooms. Hotel open all year.

TAMNIÈS 24620

Hôtel-Restaurant Laborderie. Tel. 53 29 68 59
Lovely house in a charming old village on a hilltop. Swimming pool and garden. 14 km (9 miles) from Sarlat and Les Eyzies. Meals served on the terrace. Famous for regional specialities. Excellent value for money. 32 rooms. Closed from 4 Nov to 23 Mar.

THIVIERS 24800

Hôtel France et Russie. Tel. 53 55 17 80
Rather chic hotel at the bottom of a garden. 11 comfortable rooms. Open all year round.

79

THONAC 24290

Hôtel-Restaurant Archambeau. Tel. 53 50 73 78
Family-run hotel in a modern Périgord house just outside Le Thot (Prehistoric Museum). View over the Vézère. Service on the terrace. Traditional cuisine. 16 rooms. Closed from 1 Nov to 1 Dec.

TOURTOIRAC 24390

Hôtel-Restaurant des Voyageurs. Tel. 53 51 12 29
Quiet hotel beside the Auvézère 7 km (4 miles) from the château of Hautefort. Warm welcome. Périgord cuisine. 12 clean and pleasant rooms. Open all year round.

TRÉMOLAT 24510

Hôtel-Restaurant Le Panoramic. Tel. 53 22 80 42
A modern Périgord-style house with a fantastic view over the Cingle de Trémolat. Regional cooking with imagination. 24 rooms. Closed 4 Jan to 24 Feb.

VILLEFRANCHE-DU-PÉRIGORD 24550

Hôtel-Restaurant La Cle des Champs. Tel. 53 29 95 94
Right in the heart of the country, close to the châteaux of Biron and Bonaguil. Very good local cuisine. Swimming pool with terrace. Tennis courts. 13 rooms. Open all year round.

VILLERÉAL 47210

Hôtel-Restaurant Moulin de Labique. Tel. 53 01 63 90
Charming, friendly welcome. Swimming pool. Excellent traditional cuisine. Horse-drawn carriage rides and horse-riding. Open all year round.

VITRAC 24200

Hôtel-Restaurant Plaisance. Tel. 53 28 33 04
Lovely Périgord house with a garden beside the Dordogne and a swimming pool. Meals served on the terrace. Regional cooking. 42 excellent rooms. Closed 20 Nov to 1 Feb.

Périgord Pourpre

Bastides, which appeared all over Aquitaine between the 13th and 14th centuries, represent only one aspect of this rich and diversified area: vineyards, stretching as far as the eye can see over idyllic hillsides, explain the name 'purple'. Do not neglect some particularly powerful fortresses like **Biron** and **Bonaguil**, and some glorious scenery along the Dordogne. At the very heart of the region lies the capital and third city of the Dordogne, **Bergerac**, whose very name holds promises of the south.

BERGERAC

If there were a city that could claim to have pulled itself together by an intelligent, dynamic policy of urban restoration and development, it would be Bergerac. But its small but delightful old centre had fallen into such a state of decay that indeed many a promoter would have swept the whole thing away and started again.

Bergerac lies on the River Dordogne and its role as a shipping port, particularly of wine, made it a key junction point. Its bridge, at a time when they were few and far between, gave it additional importance. Bergerac changed sides no less than six times during the Hundred Years' War, and got caught up early on in the Reformation, becoming staunchly Huguenot. At the Revocation of the Edict of Nantes, a significant part of the population emigrated to Holland or England. Today its wine and tobacco industries keep it relatively prosperous.

If you start your tour by the **port side** (the embankment is now a vast parking lot), it doesn't take much imagination to picture the flat *gabares* (barges) moored along the quays being loaded up with casks for the trip down to Bordeaux. Stroll up the rue des Récollets to the place du Docteur Cayla, a pleasant little square full of restored houses, for a look-in at the **Cloître des Récollets**. No longer a cloister, the brick and stone **81**

It could be a scene from Cyrano de Bergerac. It's his home town and the atmosphere, perfectly restored, is charmingly theatrical.

building houses the regional wine council, which checks that the quality of wines is maintained.

Plaques on the houses give details of their origins. In the maze of medieval streets you'll discover the **rue Saint-James**, with its half-timbered houses and mullioned windows, the **rue des Fontaines**, nursing its little red-brick, half-timbered

houses, including the Vieille Auberge (The Old Inn) with some 14th-century columns and capitals, as well as the **place Pélissière**, which has been so admirably restored.

In the **place de la Myrpe**, the most picturesque square of all, stands a modern statue of Cyrano de Bergerac. That was the least the town could do. For if Cyrano, a poet-musketeer, famous for his adventures as well as his extremely long nose, never actually set foot in Bergerac, he certainly put the place on the map. Every Frenchman has at least *heard* of Bergerac from the novel by Edmond de Rostand. On either side of the square stand half-timbered houses, some of them of wattle and daub, and at the end of the street that follows it lies the fascinating **Musée du Vin, de la Batellerie et de la Tonnellerie**. A long-winded name for an excellent ethno-graphical museum on three floors in one of these typical old houses, showing wine, barrel-making and ship-building techniques (same ticket as for the Musée du Tabac).

You may not be a smoker, but you cannot fail to enjoy a visit to the outstanding **Musée du Tabac** (Tobacco Museum), the only one of its kind in France. Objects and illustrations from all over the world take us on a fascinating promenade through the historical development of the habit from the Indian tribes in America to Nicot (of Nicotine

fame), who introduced it in France in 1561, till today. The museum is housed in the most beautiful of Bergerac's *hôtels*, the 17th-century Hôtel Peyrarède, in a transitional style between Renaissance and classical.

MONBAZILLAC AND THE VINEYARDS

The **château**, built in 1550, a mere 7 km (4.5 miles) out from the town, lords over carefully tended vineyards that come right up to the gates. Rectangular, with four towers, a dry moat and crenellated watch-path, Monbazillac is one of those rare châteaux that miraculously escaped damage of any sort over the centuries.

Today it is owned by the Monbazillac Wine Cooperative, made up of 200 members who are gradually enriching it with local Périgord furniture from the proceeds from visitors' tickets. As befits a château owned by wine producers, the ticket includes a glass of Monbazillac. Inside, one downstairs room is entirely devoted to a **83** little **museum** on the Huguenots. The **grand hall** has a painted ceiling and monumental chimneypiece, while the **cellars** naturally stock some of the wine and give a clear and detailed description of the special wine-making techniques employed at Monbazillac (only four other regions produce sweet white wines from 'noble rot') and show a fascinating collection of fast-disappearing utensils and equipment.

The village of **Saint-Michel-de-Montaigne** is charming. The château, alas, something of a 19th-century pastiche of the one which burned in 1884. Nevertheless, it is a moving pilgrimage to travel the 40-odd km (25 miles) west from Bergerac and 'visit' Montaigne's home (1533–92), surely one of the greatest thinkers and erudite humanists this world has ever seen. He meditated and wrote in the peace of his spartan *librairie* (study), at the top of the **Tour des Essais**, thankfully spared by the fire. It has stayed much the way it was, with some 54 of Montaigne's **84** chosen maxims (many taken from Greek authors and the Bible) engraved on the beams. Also visible are his bedroom and the chapel.

BASTIDE COUNTRY

It has become a tourist 'plus' to be a *bastide*, so that a good number of towns around are self-proclaimed *bastides*. In fact, these 'new towns' had to obey certain prescriptions and follow precise architectural requirements.

Any tour of the *bastides* should take in Monpazier (English) and Monflanquin (French), but of course there's a broad choice between Eymet, Issigeac, Castillonnès, Villeréal, Beaumont, Molières, Lalinde and a host of others in size, quality of preservation and sheer interest. To vary the pace, you might want to add two castles on the way, both quite exceptional, Biron and Bonaguil and perhaps the Renaissance Château de Lanquais near the Dordogne.

Monpazier lies on a rise above the River Dropt and is the best-preserved *bastide* of

One-Up-Town-Ship

Both the English and French had the idea of attracting inhabitants, for defence or trade reasons, to places where there were few villagers. To encourage pioneers to settle, they were exempted from military service and even some taxes.

To be a *bastide* a town had to be *'a novo'*, i.e., constructed on completely unbuilt land. The act of foundation was sealed by a contract called a *paréage*, made between the king, represented by his local delegate, and the owner of the land, the local lord or abbey. This act stipulated that the rights, dues and income from the *bastide* were to be shared equally between the founder and the owner of the land. The statute of the future inhabitants was defined: the lord committed himself to protect them and give them a *charte de coutumes*, laying down their rights and duties. The *bastide* was granted its own mini-constitution and elected its representatives, the *consuls*.

There were also architectural rules to respect: regular and geometric town planning; identical houses; economic use of space; the main façades giving onto the *carreyras* (main streets), the backs of houses onto the *carreyrous* (back lanes) and straight streets crisscrossing at right angles in a chequered fashion, leading to a central square. This in turn was bordered by arcades (*cornières* or *couverts)* and had a covered market *(halles)* in the centre. The sturdy fortress-church nearby would play a role in defence and a well-fortified curtain wall, studded with gates, normally ringed the town. The site selected would be on a hilltop ideal for visibility and defence. A space (*andronne*) would often be left between houses to prevent the spread of fire – and for rubbish disposal and latrines.

Of course, not all the *bastides* were built on exactly the same pattern, but any town built between 1229 and the beginning of the Hundred Years' War in 1350 is *not* necessarily a *bastide* – whatever the city councillors would have us believe.

85

all – which is a miracle considering it changed hands five times in the Hundred Years' War. On the hills in the distance lies its 'enemy' *bastide* Monflanquin and the Château de Biron. The act founding it was signed by Edward I of England on January 7th, 1284, represented by his seneschal Jean de Grailly, but Edward came in person to inspect it two years later. His aim, by building *bastides* at Beaumont, Molières and Monpazier, was to build his 'Maginot line', preventing the French taking

an army through the Périgord to the Agen area.

In spite of plagues, famines and roving bands of starving looters, the *bastide* remained intact until 1637 when the *croquant* leader Buffarot, a local weaver, camped at Monpazier in 1637 with 8,000 angry peasants. He was drawn and quartered in the town two months

Montbazillac can claim not only a fine sweet white wine, but also an unscathed château.

later beside the covered market (*halle*s), which still stands, its rafters without a cobweb and its old scales for regulating the weight of grain still present.

Visit the fortified 14th–15th century Gothic **church** (partly remodelled around 1550), set apart from the square as 'regulations' required. Take note of the whimsical choir stalls. Beside the church is the so-called **Maison du Chapitre** (Chapter House), probably used as a tithe barn, with lovely arched doorways and tiers of windows on each floor.

Beaumont, 16 km (10 miles) away, was started in 1272 in the form of an 'H' (for Henry III – in memory of Edward's father). As grand, if not grander than Monpazier in its day, not much of the *bastide* itself remains: a few arcades, the Lizier Gate out through the former ramparts and some Gothic houses. However, apart from its overall charm, the town has retained one major feature: the

Eglise Saint-Front, perhaps the most fetching of all the 'military' churches of the Périgord. Its four towers, connected by a parapet walk, seem to emerge straight out of a medieval castle, there for protection, rather than spiritual restoration.

The *bastide* of **Molières** was initiated by Jean de Grailly but never completed; one rather forlorn arcaded house stands on the square somehow waiting for the others to be joined to it. Nevertheless, it has an old 12th-century château and an outsize church. **Lalinde**, also an English *bastide* beside the Dordogne, has only kept a few vestiges of the outer wall, bordering the river.

 South and west of Monpazier lay the French *bastides*, but we first pass before **Biron**, the largest castle in the Dordogne – and that's saying something. The château belonged to one family, the Gontauts, for 24 generations. Many family members altered, added or adapted (and later subtracted) parts of the château so that the motley mixture of architectural **88** styles is complicated to follow

– but, for all that, it's arguably one of the great moments of a Dordogne visit.

The very oldest parts are those Simon de Montfort left upright after he had trapped the Cathar Martin d'Algaïs in the château in 1212. He first had the victim dragged by his feet behind a horse, then hanged. The château changed hands and loyalties several times during the Hundred Years' War and suffered considerably but Pons de Gontaut-Biron, who had participated in military campaigns in Italy, decided to transform his warlike castle into the 'new' Renaissance style. To him we owe the lovely collegial chapel and Renaissance loggia to which he added the mullioned windows. As the Gontauts' political role increased, so did their fortune and more and more grandiose projects were conceived, but not all completed.

Bonaguil is somewhere you would come miles to see: it is stunning, not only for its site overlooking other hills and its picture-book medieval castle look, but for its mystery. For

*M*onpazier is a well-preserved bastide and a pretty town.

why, when feudal castles were out, should the proud Seigneur Bérenger de Roquefeuil have constructed this perfectly anachronistic castle in 1490 at a time when graceful Chambord was being built? For Bonaguil is a castle, not a château. He claimed it could never be taken; he was right, it was never attacked. But it was, alas, seriously plundered over the years. And why, secondly,

did he choose to build a castle of such dimensions so far from any major crossroads?

Coming from the south, its sudden apparition on the top of a hill is simply breathtaking. Of red-and-yellow stone, with *lauze* stone roofing, and no less than 13 towers of all heights and shapes, the castle looks inviolable: in some respects, the noble lord had seen ahead of his time and the prow-shape of the château give an enemy's artillery difficult angles of fire. With over 100 artillery firing ramps, his cannon could take aim with impunity at targets anywhere. **89**

_M_agnificent from afar, imposing close to, Bonaguil is the kind of
90 château to raise gasps of admiration and merits a full half-day visit.

Sited on a sloping peak 180 m (590 ft) above the River Lède, the bastide of **Monflanquin** has retained its original, essentially defensive, plan. Its 13th–15th-century houses and arcades on stout pillars surround the small but charming **main square**. The *halles* have disappeared, but a market is still held on Thursday as it has been for seven centuries. All the roads cut each other at right angles, and each square 'block' of houses is the same size. A perfect *bastide*, in fact.

By intent, *bastides* were more or less on the same model, but it's not true to say that if you've see one, you've seen them all. **Villeréal** (founded by the Count of Toulouse in 1269) is a good example on a very small scale, with a church resembling that at Monflanquin, with brick houses and a mixture of wood and stone arcades. Its covered market with age-old wooden pillars and a circular staircase 'upstairs' is particularly appealing. **Castillonnès** stands out as a refined and remarkably early *bastide*: Alphonse de Poitiers signed the act of *paréage* in 1259 with the Abbey of Cadouin and the lords of Lanquais, who owned the land; six years later, they received their charter of *coutumes* instituting Tuesday as market day. It still is. The **place des Cornières** and the **18th-century house** on rue du Petit-Paris are worth a detour. **Eymet** has a remarkably well-preserved square with nearly all its arcades still standing, a fountain in the centre and an interesting keep-cum-museum. Especially lively is the Thursday morning market, Eymet being considered second after Sarlat as a canning town for *foie gras*. **Issigeac** is more a *bastide* in theory than in practice (no rectilinear streets or arcaded square any more), but as a town it is a pure delight, with picturesque old houses down every narrow winding lane, discoveries and details at every turn. You can't miss the 17th-century **Château des Evêques** at the entrance to the town nor the Maison de la Dîme (now housing the Tourist Office) opposite. **91**

Excursions

When is an excursion not an excursion? When it's on the doorstep of one's home base: such as **Padirac**, the greatest chasm in France and possibly Europe.

Nothing outside quite prepares you for this descent into the bowels of the earth. To begin with a lift takes you down past wild, flourishing vegetation. By the second lift, it's starting to get more barren, with drops of water splattering on your head. A vast eerie gash in the centre of the earth opens up in the third lift. After a short walk, you are invited to step aboard a punt for some 500 m (1,640 ft) along the well-lit canal and then you emerge into a 'cathedral' of such proportions (60 m-/197-ft tall) and beauty that you are spellbound. The guide's voice echoes around this décor of monstrous stalagmites and stalactites and rocks that take on uncanny forms.

Queues in summer have become inevitable, but it's worth it for the one-hour visit; some have themselves photographed in the punts, others flee the commercialization. Take binoculars and something warm and waterproof with you.

ROCAMADOUR

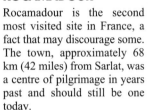

Rocamadour is the second most visited site in France, a fact that may discourage some. The town, approximately 68 km (42 miles) from Sarlat, was a centre of pilgrimage in years past and should still be one today.

Making use of natural features, Rocamadour is a town that was nailed right into the face of a cliff, defying the laws of gravity, quite apart from those of logic. Simply put, it is on three levels: a medieval tradesmen-craftsmens' city level, an ecclesiastical city level and a château level, with a good climb (on foot mostly, though there are lifts now) between each. You can start at the top and work your way down (the pilgrims did) or vice versa. For a breathtaking view of the whole, approach via L'Hospitalet or, from the Corniche de Couzou opposite, wait for nightfall and see the simply amazing spectacle of the whole rock face lit up.

COLLONGES-LA-ROUGE

As the wild and barren Massif Central slowly gives way to the more gentle countryside of the Creuse and Périgord, a remarkable little village lies just off the main road, a halt for pilgrims on their way to Compostela. Collonges-la-Rouge is what it says – a village where every mansion, house, church or barn is built in a deep red, even purple sandstone. Owing to its popularity in the late 16th century as a retreat from the heat of the plain, sumptuous manor houses and little palaces, with refined sculpture and turrets, were constructed, giving the village a fairy-tale skyline. It's so small, you've wandered around it in a hour; but stop at the **church** (much of it 11th and 12th century with a beautiful *white* Carennac stone tympanum), the **Castel de Vassignac**, with its pepperpot towers and turrets, and at the **Maison de la Sirène** with

the sculpted mermaid combing her hair with one hand and looking at herself in the mirror in the other.

SAINT-CIRQ-LAPOPIE

The name is attractive but not as pretty as Saint-Cirq-Lapopie really is, a crazy village straggling down a cliff side beside the spectacular River Lot, its church walls teetering above the waters below. There was no limit to what those daring medieval town planners would do and no bounds to their imagination and artistic sense. One of France's greatest modern poets and an experienced traveller, André Breton, put it this way: 'I ceased to wish to be elsewhere'. The village is the ultimate in beauty: its impregnable site, the vertical cliffs and the meander in the Lot, its houses with their deep brown roofs, its church, châteaux ruins, flowered gardens and steep narrow streets contribute to an effect so powerful that the visitors are few and far between who do not let out a gasp of admiration at first sight. **93**

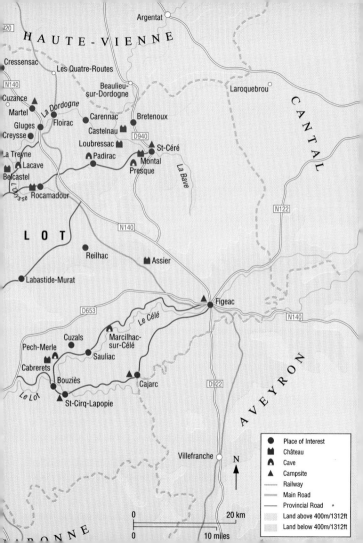

The site is stunning, but Saint-Cirq Lapopie has far more to offer. Enjoy the fantastic views over the Lot and soak up the atmosphere.

Few villages have kept such a fantastically unified street as the **Grand'Rue**, where the houses of the 13th–15th centuries come together as one, aided by artists and art-lovers who have done everything to keep it that way and restore where possible. The corbelled façades, the Gothic or Renaissance mullioned windows and the artisans' shop fronts (mostly souvenir shops today) plunge a visitor right back into the Middle Ages. Break off at **place Cayrol** for a look over the River Lot and carry on to the 15th-century fortified **sanctuary-church** on its rock-terrace. The belfry tower, somewhat stocky, is accompanied by a delightful round turret. If you have time before leaving, return to the central **place du Sombral** to investigate the **Rocher Lapopie**, with its giddying views of the village itself, the church and the apparently sedate River Lot wending its way past the *chemin de halage* (barge tow path).

PECH-MERLE

Four km (2.5 miles) out of lovely Cabrerets lies Pech-Merle, one of the most intriguing of all the prehistoric caves found so far: it allies rock formations and paintings, signs of man's presence so tangible (like children's footprints stamped for eternity in the *gour* clay) that 19,000 years ago seem like yesterday. What's more, a brilliant museum (**Musée Amédée-Lemozi**), that a visitor is encouraged to study *before* going round the caves, gives a helpful introduction to prehistory.

In 1922 two fourteen-year olds, carried away by the excitement of adventure, crept down a small fault blocked by concretions and discovered this richly decorated cave. Deep and ramified, the tour of nearly two hours (maximum of 25 per group) takes a visitor through over a mile of galleries on various levels. If the 60-odd drawings don't reach the perfection of Lascaux, the artists used the amazing natural decor to great effect.

The **Salle des Mammouths** offers a frieze of bison and mammoth, while nearby the famous silhouettes of two **horses** (*chevaux ponctués*) outlined with black dots and the '**negative hands**' (feminine hands placed against the wall outlined or stencilled, probably by a blowpipe technique, against the rock) are most moving. Horses, bears and humans are depicted. The drawings were made at different times over a *5,000-year* period. The mineral concretions in the **Salle des Disques**, where scientifically inexplicable mineral disks formed, will fascinate all, as will the huge columns and shapes of the rocks and the cave pearls.

97

What to Do

Do not hesitate to use the services of the local tourist offices, particularly in Périgueux (see p. 53), which are well equipped to deal with requests to join in organized activities or even tailor them to your needs.

Sports

'Green' holidays have become a permanent feature for many people, with **hiking** enabling peaceful exercise. Every *Syndicat d'Initiative* (Tourist Office) will provide you with itineraries, highlighting some local and 'national' routes (*Sentiers de Grandes Randonnées*). The paths are marked in red and white on trees, rocks or whatever comes to hand. If you want to join a group, there are guided tours on foot. Bring along a pair of proper walking shoes (they're even useful for visiting caves). The detailed IGN maps are ideal and available at any bookshop (or else contact the Comité départe-mental des Sentiers de Grandes Randonnées, Résidence Vésu-na, 7, Impasse Vésone, 24000 Périgueux).

If you are interested in **speleology** (the study of caves), there are plenty of options available: contact the local group at 7, rue de la Cité, 24000 Périgueux or else the Tourist Office. The Musée de la Spéléologie at Les Eyzies-de-Tayac (tel. 53 29 78 42) can give practical advice. There are also rock-climbing and speleology courses organized at Cénac (tel. 53 28 22 01).

The Dordogne is a paradise for **cyclists**: miles of almost car-free lanes, with spectacular views. You can hire bikes virtually in any town and at railway stations (see p. 119). You may want to join up with others to get the maximum out of cycling: the Comité départe-mental de cyclotourisme et cyclo-assistance, 51, rue Jean Mermoz, 24000 Chamiers (tel. 53 09 08 22) will certainly be able to help.

From Saint-Avit-de-Vialard and elsewhere you can rent a **donkey** and advice is offered concerning where to stop, routes to take and what to feed the animal. Don't expect to go great distances – but what a relief not to have to carry your own baggage. The same goes for a **horse and carriage**, that can be hired with a driver for a day or a week from Lisle, or else without a driver, but a real wagon (*roulotte*), from Issigeac or Quinsac.

The Dordogne is an excellent area for horse-riding: *stages* (courses) are offered everywhere, with *randonnées* (excursions) through the lovely countryside including stops at specially equipped country *auberges* (inns). For more details contact Tourisme Équestre de la Dordogne, 4–6, place Francheville, 24000 Périgueux (tel. 53 09 26 26).

Canoeing (*canoë-kayak*) is a major sport on the Dordogne and Vézère rivers, offered at many points. To see the country as our prehistoric ancestors did, what better way than to paddle down the Vézère from Montignac to Trémolat? To see the castles along the Dordogne, why not hire a canoe at Cénac or Beynac? For rougher stuff, the Auvézère and the upper parts of the Isle, Loue and Dronne offer some thrills. Réservation Loisirs Accueil in the Tourist Office in Périgueux (see Tourist Offices p. 142) will arrange a tailor-made excursion and advise on which rivers – and where.

Golf is an up-and-coming sport. You can tee off at Périgueux-Marsac (9 holes), the Château de Sadillac (9 holes), Castelnaud (27 holes) or at Siorac (9 holes), where lessons are given by an instructor.

Helicopter **flights** over the Dordogne area are possible with Héli-Dordogne at Sarlat-Domme Aerodrome (tel. 53 28 24 36 – English spoken). You can choose between flights over 9 or 32 castles or Rocamadour and a 17-châteaux circuit (if you want to see the *bastides* from the air, ring 53 36 85 99). **Parachuting** can be attempted from Bergerac's Roumanières Aerodrome, and the Tourist Office offers a week's course with 10 jumps. **Hot-air ballooning** (*montgolfières*) is organized from the Château de Veyrignac. **99**

Of course, some summer days are sizzling hot, so everyone wants a **swim**. Luckily, there are pools (*piscines*) beside the rivers and in the nu-merous lakes (*étang*). Camping sites are sometimes equipped with **tennis** courts, as are all the big towns. If you want to **fish** on the Dordogne you can

*T*he Dordogne comes into its own with miles of rivers for exciting canoeing and fermes d'auberge offering excursions on horseback.

take a short weekend course with an instructor and eat your catch for dinner. You can fish in the rivers such as the Auvézère for trout, carp, roach or tench, or the lakes such as Born or Rouffiac. However, a pass is obligatory (check with the *Syndicat d'Initiative*).

Other Activities. 'Activities' centred around eating or food products are a must in this gastronomic paradise. These range from enlightening visits to museums (Thiviers, foie gras; Sorges, the truffle; Villefranche-du-Périgord, the chestnut, walnut and mushroom), to practical weekend courses at Villefranche (getting to know the various types of mushrooms and their properties), to learning the secrets of Périgord cuisine on farms at Saint-Crépin-et-Carlucet or Baneuil or how best to put the truffle to use at Sorges. There's also a garlic festival in Rouffignac at the end of July and a wine festival at Cénac in August. You will be invited to watch the manufacturing process, taste the result and buy home-made farm products from foie gras to honey wherever you go – not to mention wine-tastings around Bergerac. **101**

Shopping

Style means everything in France, from the humblest pâtisserie wrapping to the shape of a tin of *foie gras complet*. Variety, too, is the order of the day: you don't ask for bread, but *baguette, ficelle* or *pain de campagne*; no plain ham here but *jambon de Bayonne, jambon de York, torchon* or *jambon de montagne*. It's fun to watch the housewives haggling and comparing merits at the market: they want the best and at the right price, of course.

SHOPPING HOURS

Most shops open Tuesday to Saturday from 8 or 9 a.m. to noon and from 2 to 7 p.m. Bakeries open before other shops, and there's practically always a small grocer (*épicerie*) in the bigger towns where you can get everything till 9 or even 10 p.m. On Sundays, too, you are rarely stuck, even if food shops mostly close at midday.

WHERE TO SHOP

The best prices and the biggest choice can be had at the *hypermarchés* and *supermarchés* (hyper-and supermarkets) lying on the outskirts of town. Markets are more fun, and in most towns they have had them for centuries on the same day. The goose market in Sarlat is par-

Good food is a supreme ingredient in the Périgord. The assortment on offer can overwhelm.

ticularly lively. Department stores (*grandes surfaces*) only exist in Périgueux. If it's presents you're after, try one of the local artisan-craft shops advertised in the *Syndicat d'Initiative* (Tourist Office); they are concentrated in tourist centres (Monpazier, Saint-Cirq-Lapopie, Brantôme, Sarlat), but sell some good creative items. Many shops displaying the sign 'Qualité Accueil Périgord' have signed a charter guaranteeing that they won't 'rip off' a client. Luckily, in the Dordogne that's rare anyway.

WHAT TO BUY

Antiques. *Brocantes* (second-hand shops) abound, and if you're looking for inexpensive items to give cheer and originality to your house, this is the best place to try. Serious antique dealers with bigger pieces in walnut (the Dordogne wood) are found in the most popular tourist towns (La Roque-Gageac, Monpazier). A visit to a *vente aux enchères* (auction), advertised in the local press, on walls and at the Hôtel des

egional specialities include pâté de foie gras and truffes, expensive but worth the hunt.

Ventes (auction house), provides local colour as well as occasional bargains. See Antique Fairs, p. 107.

Ceramics. Potters of all nationalities have set up in the Dordogne (Mussidan, Sarlat and Le Moustier), and their wares are often distinctive and **103**

highly personal. Although there is no specific regional style, themes inspired by discoveries from the caves are often used.

Cheeses. The *cabécous*, tiny round goat cheeses, best from Rocamadour but found everywhere, are light and easy to pack. Le *Trappe Echourgnac* or *Saint-Heblon*, genuine Dordogne cheeses, also make good souvenirs.

Crafts (in general). At summer craft exhibitions a range of products is sold (Saint-Amand-de-Coly). In Périgueux, the rue Aubergerie is a crafts centre, while there is a gallery specializing in wrought-iron work at Ribérac. Saint-Jean-de-Côle has a gallery offering just about every craft you can imagine.

Farm products. From the major industrial brands to the local farmers advertising their own wares, you are spoilt for choice. With the big names, the standard is guaranteed but sometimes the taste is a little bland; with the local farmer, the taste can sometimes be *too* local but it might have that extra something you're looking for.

Not only is *foie gras* found in all shapes and sizes but there are many other tinned Périgord specialities, often decidedly less dear: *terrines de canard, rillettes d'oie, fritons de canard, terrine campagnarde truffée, bloc de foie gras de canard avec morceaux truffés, cou farci au foie gras, confits de canard,* etc. They often come in delightful earthenware jars and canisters. Why not take back a jar of *graisse d'oie* (goose fat) to prepare some of the dishes that require this special fat? Farmers often prepare a gift package (*lot cadeau*) of a variety of their specialities. You can find all the products in countless shops in Périgueux, Le Bugue and Sarlat, but also 'grouped' as at the covered market in Les Eyzies.

Glass blowing *(souffleur de verre)*. Not a particular Dordogne speciality but there are a few around, some that prepare exactly what you ask for (such as at Limeuil). It makes a very personal and handsome present. The same goes for stained glass (at Mussidan, for instance).

*D*espite competition from supermarkets, local markets still carry on. For quality food, the French won't skimp on price.

Honey *(miel)*. You probably didn't think of the Dordogne for honey, but it's excellent. Again, there is a Musée d'Apiculture (Museum of Apiculture) and plenty of producers to choose from.

Minerals. There is quite a trade in minerals, carved into ornaments and very decorative pieces of jewellery.

Paper. Traditionally along the Dordogne around Couze there has always been paper-making. Look for beautiful hand-made paper.

Porcelain. Limoges is very close and its influence can be felt. You'll find good outlets for inimitable De Havilland and other porcelain, mostly in Périgueux and Nontron.

Prunes *(pruneaux)*. The real region for prunes is nearby Agen, but they're also sold near Eymet.

Spirits *(eaux de vie)*. A few distilleries struggle on for survival against the 'international' manufacturers: at Villambard a firm that's been going since 1834 sells liqueurs (peach, apricot, strawberry, nut) and spirits (plum, raspberry, pear, plum brandy) and will organize visits. You'll notice apéritifs and spirits with a nut base everywhere.

Walnuts. Far more tasty than their nearest rivals from Grenoble, let alone from overseas.

Walnut oil *(huile vierge de noix et de noisettes)*. The oil dressing on a salad can immediately make it more interesting; try the Périgord walnut oil, you'll be surprised. At Sainte-Nathalène near Sarlat, you can visit the mill and watch the manufacturing process.

Wines. Nowadays you find everything everywhere, but why not take back your own Bergerac wine that you bought while wine-tasting in the winegrowers cellar? Most bergeracs, reds and rosés, are good local wines, drunk young and very reasonably priced.

Entertainment

The Dordogne excels in **summer festivals**, mostly music, but also dance and theatre.

Brantôme uses its caves with the sculpted rock frescoes for a dance festival in midsummer. Biron also has a dance festival in July–August. Rocamadour, Cadouin and Bonaguil offer spectacular sound-and-light shows in the summer months. Montignac goes in for folklore and holds its festival in July. Sarlat uses its natural décor and numerous churches for plays and concerts, while Saint-Amand-de-Coly holds an annual music festival in late July that is gaining an international reputation. Périgueux specializes in mime and has its own festival in August, Souillac concentrates on jazz in both July and August, as does Bergerac in the Cloître des Récollets.

There is scarcely a town or castle that does not contribute something to the cultural scene during the summer, be it the evocation of a castle's history in a sound-and-light show or a tiny village like Fanlac celebrating Jacquou le Croquant. As dates and times constantly change, for your day-to-day selections you'll need to obtain the Tourist Office's brochure 'Le Périgord en fête' which gives a complete rundown. The English-language bi-monthly Dordogne Telegraph is most helpful, too.

There are also other types of fair. **Antique Fairs** are held at Belvès in July and August (more *brocante*, in fact) for those with an eye for digging out the unusual and Lamothe-Montravel has a bric-à-brac and antique fair (the distinction isn't always clear) in July and August. Bergerac, not to be left out, has its fair in July, with the exchange of old car parts in November.

Rocamadour attracts thousands of visitors for its famous **pilgrimage** on September 8th. It's best to book a room in advance if you do not want to stay too far out.

The Dordogne is not really the place for sophisticated **nightlife**, although Sarlat, Périgueux and Bergerac cater for those who want to live it up. Discos are often sited outside towns to avoid disturbance, but remember, this is not the Côte d'Azur. However, there are scores of *bals populaires* (on July 14th they're literally everywhere) where you don't necessarily have to be a great dancer to join in the fun.

One **fête** unique to the Périgord whose origins go back into the mists of time is the Félibrée, where a different town each year in the *département* is chosen to hold a great folkloric get-together in traditional dress with dancing, decorations and singing.

Outside the summer season (October to May), festivals and fairs are far more infrequent, but there are the most 'genuine' **markets** at Sarlat and Périgueux and Thiviers in November – if markets can be considered entertainment. **107**

Eating Out

The very name Périgord makes you think of good cuisine, succulent, plentiful, the height of gastronomic art. It's normally a hearty, country cuisine with marvellous products – refined by chefs with imagination and talent, often best tasted at country farms.

BREAKFAST

French breakfasts tend to be summary affairs, with bread, butter, jam, croissants and a pot of coffee, tea or a cup of hot chocolate. Of late, this has changed – orange juice, cornflakes, toast and other innovations have appeared. This has allowed some hoteliers to raise the price of their breakfasts to almost that of a decent meal. It's much more fun (and less expensive) to go to the local bar for a *petit noir* (a small black coffee) and croissant. You'll watch a town come to life, the locals coming in to take a quick coffee, glance at the paper and rush off to work. Incidentally, a majority of Frenchmen avoid *café crème* (coffee with milk or cream) – it's considered filling and kills the taste of the coffee.

LUNCH

Lunch used to be as important if not more so than dinner; even if today the trend is towards a light, easily digestible lunch without wine. However, on holiday a large lunch is definitely permissible. After all, you can always treat yourself to a siesta afterwards. Hamburger stalls, fast-food outlets, pizzerias, *saladeries* (salad shops) and *crêperies* (pancake parlours) flourish, to the chagrin of purists, while standard restaurants offer a *plat du jour* (dish of the day) to lure customers short of time. Bistros provide sandwiches a foot long, with often more bread than filling, or somewhat insipid plastic-wrapped *croque-monsieur*s (cheese on toast) at any time (*à toute heure*). Many restaurants also propose just a salad for a hot summer day – *salade au cabécou* (goat cheese salad), for instance.

Between noon and 12.30 p.m. you do not have to book a table; after that it might get crowded if it's a popular place. After 1.45 p.m. you run the risk of being refused a meal, although this is less common in summer.

If you don't fancy staying indoors on a lovely day, the sheer choice in a good *charcuterie* or *traiteur* – cold meats, pâtés, terrines, *rillettes d'oie* or *de canard*, salads, dishes prepared that day or grated vegetables – will surely tempt you. The *charcuteries* in the supermarkets have a large (but industrially produced) selection. Be careful, though – before you know it, you can find yourself paying as much for your picnic items as for a full sit-down meal. With your meat, cheese and salad, a *baguette* (French stick) under your arm, not forgetting some local Bergerac wine or cider, all that remains

is to find your spot. And that, in the Dordogne, is rarely a problem.

DINNER

After a full sightseeing programme, a refreshing dinner is just what the doctor would prescribe. In summer dinner can be served until late, but usually 8 or 8.30 p.m. is about right. After 9.30 p.m. there may be some raised eyebrows.

A café terrace can be as simple as a couple of chairs outside an arcade.

To enable you to choose, there is a mass of literature, but it's sometimes hard to distinguish advertising from reality. If you can get over the language barrier, ask local people ('*Pouvez-vous me recommander un bon restaurant pas trop cher?*'), even if you have to use sign language. Locals always know which restaurant has the edge. Tourist offices hesitate to recommend one establishment over another.

For your main meat dish, you'll expect it to be less well done than in some countries – extra rare is *bleu*, rare *saignant*, medium *à point* and well done *bien cuit*. The latter is sometimes so looked down upon that on some menus it is

A taste of Dordogne specialities, including the ever-prized truffles and boletus mushrooms.

FRENCH FOOD

The *hors d'oeuvre* – often a simple dish like *crudités* (salad), or an *assiette de charcuterie* (a selection of cold meats) – are there to whet the appetite. Salads that came between meat and cheese are now often starters. *Charcuterie,* particularly in the Dordogne, could be home-made terrine or *rillettes* (a soft pâté usually of duck or sometimes goose meat or pork), various kinds of sausage and ham. On a cold day a *potage* (soup), such as *potage aux légumes* (usually leek and potato based), can be simply delicious.

110

solemnly announced that meat will *not* be prepared 'well done'.

The Dordogne does not have many of its own cheeses, except for the Saint-Heblon and Trappe Echourgnac. However, the Lot's goat cheese from Rocamadour, the little *cabécou*, is tasty and available everywhere.

As you're on holiday, why not indulge in a fattening dessert? On offer are heavenly *mousse au chocolat*, *profiteroles* (delicious ball-shaped éclairs filled with vanilla ice cream and coated with hot chocolate sauce) and fruit tarts.

Although it may not be on the menu displayed outside a restaurant, there should be house wines (*réserve du patron*) at affordable prices. A wine list with only grand names can turn a reasonable meal into a wickedly expensive one. This is not often the case in the Dordogne where standard Bergeracs are not expensive and even Pécharmants, a cut above, are reasonable. House wines or wine in a **111** *carafe* or *pichet* are usually acceptable, sometimes delicious. If you don't want wine or mineral water, state firmly: '*une carafe d'eau, s'il vous plaît*': there's no obligation to have wine or bottled mineral water.

REGIONAL SPECIALITIES

Goose or duck takes pride of place on the Périgord table. A typical main dish would be *confit d'oie* (or *de canard*) *aux pommes salardaises* (goose preserved in its own fat, browned, with potatoes also cooked in goose dripping). The luxury version adds truffles to these *pommes salardaises*, that accompany many a dish in the area. You will often see specialities such as *cou d'oie farci sur son lit de pommes* (stuffed goose neck with apples), *aiguillettes de canard au vinaigre de framboise* (fillet of duck in raspberry vinegar), *civet de gésiers et sa poire au vin* (goose gizzards with pear in wine). Pheasants (*faisan*) and game often appear. Chicken, turkey and pork (though often called an *enchaud*) are also

prepared as *confits*. *Magrets* are also often seen (fillet breast of fattened duck grilled or fried and served rare) in such preparations as *magret de canard au citron vert* (fillet of duck in lime sauce). The mushrooms (*chanterelles, morilles, cèpes*) frequently come into play with the meats, as *canard farci aux cèpes* (duck stuffed with boletus mushrooms*)* or *perdrix aux morilles* (partridge with morels).

The Périgord family by tradition has *tourain (*soup) with every meal, three times a day. It comes in various forms, such as *tourain* (or *tourin*) *à l'ail* or *tourain blanchi* (with garlic). In summer a *salade aux lardons* or *aux gésiers* (with gizzards) might be the refreshing starter you're looking for. Next might come (it could be either/or) the grandiose *foie gras au torchon mi-cuit* with lightly grilled bread, a *mousse de foie d'oie* (goose liver mousse) or simply pâté. Often duck (*canard*), that some people consider more tasty if less refined (and less expensive) than goose *(oie)*, is proposed. The

*E*ven today, the final touch to canning pâté is done by hand.

pâté is often '*aux truffes*', speckled with truffles: unless the latter are absolutely first-rate, one can justifiably ask whether they add that much – except to the bill. Truffles, becoming rarer and rarer, are of course essential in certain preparations. Don't miss a chance to have an *omelette aux truffes* (truffle omelette), where the bigger pieces are likely to leave a stronger taste and aroma. The delicious *omelettes aux cèpes* (with boletus mushrooms) figure on most menus.

Fish enters Périgord cuisine with crayfish *à la périgourdine*, cooked as one would expect in goose dripping, and local trout, often as a soufflé or cooked in Monbazillac wine.

In the unlikely event that you tire of fowl, there are plenty of specialities such as *cassoulet*; if you thought it only came from Toulouse, you'll be interested in the Périgord variety with its preserved duck.

There will be plenty of standard, less 'regional' dishes such as *émincé de boeuf aux morilles* (beef stew with morels), *filet mignon au poivre vert* (pork with green pepper sauce) or steaks prepared in various ways. Tournedos Rossini (a tender slice of beef with *foie gras* and truffles) – although invented in Paris – has been 'adopted' by the Périgord. Stuffings (*farces*) are often used, usually with liver and truffles. As to sauces, you'll **113** see the rich *sauce Périgueux* frequently, a Madeira sauce with a drop of cognac and fresh truffles, and *rouilleuse* (with white wine, the sauce thickened with blood), particularly with chicken.

For dessert, if you can you should try a *pastis* (no, nothing to do with the drink), an apple pie (though originally plum) with flaky pastry, with a good dose of Armagnac. Dordogne's walnuts come into their own with the *gâteau aux noix:* not only exquisite, it's very filling, so keep some room for it.

DORDOGNE WINES

Most Dordogne wines come from the Bergerac area adjoining Bordeaux's Entre-Deux-Mers vineyards, although local patches of vines appear here and there. Pride of place goes to Monbazillac. Monbazillac is among the best 'liquorous' sweet white wines, an ideal accompaniment to melon, *charcuterie*, *foie gras* and desserts. It's also an apéritif for special occasions.

The standard dry white Bergerac and Montravel wines are good, fragrant and fruity and go nicely with fish (they can be drunk young); the sweet whites (Saussignac, Côtes de Montravel, Haut Montravel or Côtes de Bergerac) complement white meats. Pécharmant, little known but a full-bodied and most pleasant wine, accompanies cheese, red meat and game. It's already good after three years, reaches full maturity between five and seven but is even better after ten years. All Dordogne wines have a big advantage: their price.

Neighbouring Lot has the robust Cahors, the drink of kings in the Middle Ages, now a wine for dishes with strong tastes (game, red meats, strong cheeses). And the Coteaux du Quercy make very good picnic wines – but induce a distinct urge for a siesta afterwards.

The average Frenchman is less a big drinker than a choosy one. Generally speaking, he or she saves wine for meals. Increasingly, half bottles for two people and mineral water are drunk at lunch time.

BLUEPRINT
for a
Perfect Trip

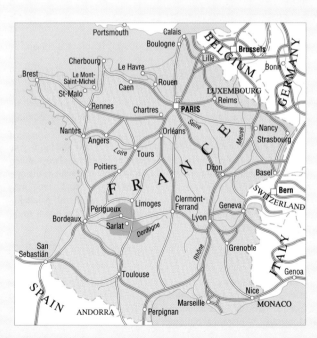

An A–Z Summary of Practical Information

Listed after most main entries is an appropriate French translation, usually in the singular. You'll find this vocabulary useful when asking for information or assistance.

A

ACCOMMODATION (See also CAMPING, YOUTH HOSTELS and the HOTEL/RESTAURANT SECTION)

Accommodation is not wildly expensive. However, in mid-summer there can be a shortage. It is advisable to book in advance or reserve a room by lunch time for that evening. You are often expected to take your evening meal in the establishment, but there is no binding obligation.

The *Syndicat d'Initiative,* (S.I.) or (I), provides lists and helps you find a suitable room. In case of emergencies, there are always other solutions which a tourist office (S.I.) will recommend such as the options listed below.Hotels are graded by stars, by national or regional official bodies (be careful not to confuse these stars with Michelin recommendations), from 5 stars equivalent to luxury down to 1, which can be a bit dubious.

TYPES OF HOTEL

Relais et Châteaux. These hotels, covering the whole of France, offer several tempting possibilities in the Lot and Dordogne. All are four- or five-star establishments, some, such as the Edward Ier in Monpazier, in historical buildings.

Relais du Silence. A chain of two- to four-star hotels in particularly tranquil settings. Some are genuine, old-time stagecoach inns. Establishments are listed in a free booklet published annually, available from the tourist office.

Logis de France. Small or medium family-run hotel-restaurants, mostly in the 1–2-star-bracket, almost all of which lie outside urban areas, in villages or in the country. The Logis de France produces an annual guide (free if requested from national tourist offices abroad).

ALTERNATIVE ACCOMMODATION

Ferme-Auberge. In the Dordogne and the Lot you can often see signposts stating 'Bienvenue à la Ferme'. A *ferme-auberge* is normally on a working farm. It is run by the farmer and members of his family. It might not always propose accommodation, but the dishes offered will be regional or local specialities, made with fresh ingredients. Lists can be acquired from any tourist office or from the Relais Agriculture et Tourisme, Chambre d'Agriculture de la Dordogne, 4 et 6, place Francheville, 24000 Périgueux; tel. 53 09 26 26.

Gîte d'Etape and Gîte de Randonnée. This type of accommodation is essentially for individual hikers or groups (walkers, horse-riders, cyclists) who want to make a break before continuing their trip. It often lies along footpaths or country lanes and functions on a nightly basis or provides a convenient midday halt.

Ferme Equestre. The *ferme équestre* is a farm where riding is practised, usually providing accommodation and meals. All types of riding are available.

Gîte et Meublé à la Ferme. The *gîte* can be a house or furnished lodging on a farm that has to conform to certain requirements.

Table d'hôte/Chambre d'hôte. Private individuals, usually in the country, offer meals and/or bed. To get a taste of France, they are well worth a try. Cooking in private homes is often better than in restaurants, and you'll get to meet some marvellous people. A *chambre d'hôte* room will include the cost of breakfast.

SELF-CATERING

Gîtes Ruraux. An official body, the Gîtes de France (with regional offices) oversees the organization and fixes the standards (Office départemental du Tourisme, Gîtes de France Dordogne/Périgord, 15 rue Wilson, 24009 Périgueux; tel. 53 53 44 35, fax 53 09 51 41).

A *gîte rural* provides self-catering holiday accommodation throughout the year. Normally speaking, they are either in old houses of regional character or else in renovated farm buildings. Certain minimal standards of comfort (running water, toilets, washing and kitchen facilities, etc.) are required. Each *gîte* is allocated to house a fixed number of guests. It is rented by the week, but the lease can be prolonged.

Do you have a single/double room for tonight?	**Avez-vous une chambre pour une/deux personnes pour cette nuit?**
with bath/shower/toilet	**avec bain/douche/toilettes**
What's the rate per night?	**Quel est le prix pour une nuit?**

BICYCLE HIRE

No one can deny that there's plenty of uphill pedalling, but what a cyclist's paradise with so many options off the beaten track. A VTT *(vélo tous terrains)* mountain bike isn't really necessary though you'll see them advertised everywhere. Suggestions of items to have with you: sun cream, an anorak, lip moistener, glucose tablets and a detailed map (IGN 47–48, IGN Dordogne or Michelin no. 75). Above all, travel light – over 10 kg (22 lbs) and those hillocks will seem like mountains!

Bikes can be hired at the SNCF (National Railways) of most large towns and are advertised *(location de vélos)* in shops. You'll need to leave a deposit that varies considerably (for the SNCF, if you have a recognized bank card or a special SNCF pass, this may be waived). Several towns have mopeds *(vélomoteurs)* or scooters for hire. All moped (and motorcycle) riders and passengers must wear crash helmets. The use of dipped headlights is obligatory at all times of day. Mopeds are not allowed on motorways. Prices can double from one rental shop to the next, so it's worth shopping around.

I would like to hire a bike, please	**J'aimerais louer un vélo, s'il vous plaît**
For half a day/a day/a week	**Pour une demi-journée/une journée/une semaine**

BOAT TRIPS

To go up the Dordogne in a *gabare* (a long, flat-bottomed boat), particularly between Beynac and Domme, gives a different perspective to the countryside and castles, helps to avoid the intractable traffic problems and can be most pleasurable. Boats leave from Beynac, La Roque-Gageac and Bergerac (tel. 53 29 40 44). Trips usually last one hour. For a trip on the Lot, boats can be hired from Cahors.

C

CAMPING

Camping is remarkably well organized and streamlined, with the odd crisis in summer due to crowds. A free catalogue 'Camping & Caravanning Dordogne-Périgord' shows what is available on each site, with addresses, telephone numbers, closing dates and amenities. It is obtainable from the Office départemental de Tourisme de la Dordogne at 16, rue Wilson, 24009 Périgueux Cédex; tel. 53 53 44 35, fax 53 09 51 41. For specific information on pitches available tel. 53 50 79 80.

About 150 camping sites are scattered all over the Dordogne (mostly in Périgord Noir at all sorts of convenient points, many near the rivers). They range from 30-odd places *(emplacements)* to huge sites in the 500–600-pitch category. They are clean and most have useful amenities (showers, swimming pool, café/restaurant, bicycle hire, tent renting facilities, etc.). Don't camp just anywhere *(camping sauvage)*; it's illegal and you could find yourselves forcibly and unpleasantly ejected at some ungodly hour. Look out for *camping à la ferme* (which means the farmer is willing to let you camp on his land and use the basic facilities). *Camping interdit* means 'no camping allowed'.

Have you room for a tent/a caravan?	**Avez-vous de la place pour une tente/une caravane?**
May we camp on your land, please?	**Pouvons-nous camper sur votre terrain, s'il vous plaît?**

CAR HIRE (location de voitures)

To hire a car, you must show your driving licence (held for at least one year) and a passport. The minimum age for hiring cars is from 20 to 23, depending on the firm – a substantial deposit (refundable) is usually required unless you hold a credit card recognized by the car-hire company, and you'll be asked for proof of your hotel or a local address. Third-party insurance is compulsory. For addresses, look in the telephone book under *Location de voitures*.

I'd like to hire a car now/tomorrow. for one day/a week.	**Je voudrais louer une voiture tout de suite/demain. pour une journée/une semaine**

CHILDREN

From dawn to dusk, the activities that interest you are likely to interest the children, too. Châteaux and prehistory fascinate them, not only the caves with drawings, but also the mysterious troglodytic dwellings, the stalactites and stalagmites and weird rock formations. Most are enthralled by the brilliantly conceived scientific display of prehistory at Le Thot and Préhisto-Parc on the road to Tursac from Les Eyzies.

If the children do grow sick of caves and châteaux, there's always a swimming pool *(piscine)* in the neighbourhood. Towns like Domme and Rocamadour have a miniature train ride; Sarlat and Le Bugue have remarkable aquariums; Rocamadour has a monkey park, and a bird of prey park, and Padirac has a zoo. Quercyland at Souillac has everything from trampolines to water-toboggans. At Martel's Reptileland you can gaze at crocodiles, lizards, tortoises and snakes, while at Payrac's Aquafolies leisure park there is every kind of aquatic pleasure. Or what about butterflies at the Butterfly Park at l'Hospitalet?

CLIMATE and CLOTHING

Although the Dordogne's climate is temperate all year round, even in summer a jumper or anorak can come in handy. In June/July you'll probably be fine in light sportswear, but warmer articles can be useful for your visits to the caves where the temperature is kept at a constant 11–13° C. Although light shoes are adequate most of the time, to walk on the uneven floors of caves, the *pisé* floors of châteaux or the cobblestones of Saint-Jean-de-Côle you are best well shod.

For the classier hotels and restaurants, casual chic is appropriate – the French appreciate, even in high summer, if some sartorial efforts are made, at least for dinner.

Summer can be really hot, between 19 and 27° C or more.

If possible, try to come to the Dordogne in May/June or September/October. Not only are there fewer problems with accommodation and crowds, but the gentleness of the climate out-of-season, **121** with temperatures between 12 and 19°C, and the more relaxed hoteliers definitely make autumn or spring the best seasons. Even in winter the climate rarely sinks below 9 to 12°C and, if attractions are curtailed, the countryside is its pristine self and some of the most important markets (Sarlat, Thenon, Thiviers) come into their own.

To get the local weather forecast – you'll probably understand the gist of the recorded message – ring 53 57 11 11.

COMPLAINTS

In general, as a foreigner, it's best not to complain too loudly about minor imperfections – it will do more harm than good, particularly if your French isn't fluent enough. Take inadequacies with tolerance, tact and the realization that what looks like inefficiency may be a traditional way of doing things. However, if you've been charged for the wrong *menu* or hotel room, you obviously have to react. If you should have reason to complain, firmness, a sense of humour and a little French are your most useful assets.

I'd like to make a complaint.   **J'ai une réclamation à faire.**

CRIME

Violent crime is most rare, but like anywhere else these days you should take elementary precautions to avoid problems. Never leave a car unlocked and if possible remove the radio and put everything in the boot. In markets, be particularly careful to watch your wallet or handbag. Car parks are especially popular with thieves. Any loss, theft or attempt at breaking into your car should be reported to the nearest *Commissariat de Police* immediately. A report is necessary for the insurance company.

CUSTOMS (douane) and ENTRY FORMALITIES

British visitors only need a passport to enter France, as do nationals of other EC countries and Switzerland. Anyone else should contact the French embassy in his or her country for information on entry requirements.

The following chart shows the main items you may take into France and, when returning home, into your own country:

Into:	Cigarettes		Cigars		Tobacco	Spirits		Wine
France 1)	200	or	50	or	250g	1L	and	2L
2)	300	or	75	or	400g	1\F(1,2)L	and	5L
3)	400	or	100	or	500g	1L	and	2L
Australia	250	or	50		250g	1L	or	1L
Canada	200	and	50	and	900g	1.1L	or	1L
Eire 1)	200	or	50	or	250g	1L	and	2L
2)	200	or	75	or	400g	1\F(1,2) L	and	5L
New Zealand	200	or	50	or	250g	1.1L	or	4½L
South Africa	400	and	50	and	250g	1L	and	2L
UK 1)	200	or	50	or	250g	1L	and	2L
2)	300	or	75	or	400g	1\F(1,2)	and	2L
USA	200	and	100	and	4)	1L	or	1L

1) Arriving from EC countries (items have been purchased duty free) or from other European countries.
2) Arriving from EC countries (duty has been paid on items).
3) Residents outside Europe.
4) A reasonable quantity.

British visitors may also bring back £120 worth of goods duty free.

Currency restrictions. There is no limit on the importation or exportation of foreign currencies or traveller's cheques, but amounts exceeding 50,000 French francs or equivalent must be declared on arrival.

I've nothing to declare.   **Je n'ai rien à déclarer.**
It's for my own use.   **C'est pour mon usage personnel.**

D

DISABLED TRAVELLERS

Although the Dordogne is not particularly wheelchair-friendly there are occasionally disabled toilets and phone boxes in towns. A change in general attitude is occurring so that at least new buildings are being tailored to the needs of the disabled.

DRIVING IN FRANCE

To take a car into France, you will need a valid driving licence, car registration papers, insurance coverage (the green card is no longer obligatory but comprehensive coverage is advisory), a red warning triangle and a set of spare bulbs.

Drivers and *all* passengers (back and front) are required by law to wear seat belts (assuming your car is equipped with them in the back). Children under 10 may not travel in the front (unless the car has no back seat). Driving on a foreign provisional licence is not permitted. The minimum age for driving is 18.

Driving regulations. Drive on the right, overtake on the left. (*Serrez à droite* means 'Keep to the right'). In built-up areas, give *automatic* priority to vehicles coming from the right. But the *priorité* rule does not apply at roundabouts called *giratoires*. Outside built-up areas – at junctions marked by signs with a cross or a yellow square on a white background – the more important of the two roads has right of way. The use of car horns in built-up areas is allowed only as a warning. At night, lights should be used for this purpose.

Speed limits. 130 kph (around 80 mph) on toll motorways, 110 kph (approximately 70 mph) on dual carriageways, 90 kph (56 mph) on country roads and 45 or 60 kph (28 or 37 mph) in built-up areas. When roads are wet, all limits are reduced by 10 kph (6 mph), except for motorways – where maximum speed in fog, rain or snow is reduced by 20 kph (12 mph). The word *rappel* in towns and villages reminds you that a speed limit is in force.

Signposting on the whole is good. Tourist sights are usually highlighted with a brown symbol. A blue road sign directs you to an *autoroute* (motorway), a green one to a *route nationale* (*RN* – main road) and a white to secondary D roads.

Road conditions. This whole area is without a motorway (though the Paris-Bordeaux-Toulouse *autoroute* passes along the Atlantic coast). The *RN*s (main roads), therefore, have to bear the brunt of the traffic.

France-Inter's *Inter-Route* service – which operates 24 hours a day from Paris – can also help. Most of the time, there is someone who speaks English. Tel 16 (1) 48 58 33 33. There's also the Centre d'Information Autoroutes, 7 bis, rue du Pont des Loges, 55007 Paris; tel. 16 (1) 47 05 90 01.

Parking (*stationnement*) is not easy in the height of summer, but not too bad the rest of the year. It's never much fun in Périgueux or Sarlat, so it's better to park outside the centre and do the maximum on foot. Most of the major tourist sights have decently sized parking areas, but small towns or overgrown villages like Montignac, Beynac or La Roque-Gageac can have problems.

You'll encounter two parking systems – *zone bleue* (blue zone) and meters. If you want to leave your car in a *zone bleue* you will need a *disque de stationnement,* a parking disc in the form of a cardboard clock which you can obtain from a petrol station or newsagent. Set it to show the time you arrived and it will indicate when you have to leave. Then display it in the car, visible through the windscreen. *Disque obligatoire* means 'Disc obligatory'. Meters are often *horodateurs:* you simply place the receipt from the machine in the car window that indicates when you are due to leave *Stationnement interdit* means 'no parking' and *Stationnement genant* means 'parking obstructive'.

Breakdowns (*en panne*). There are emergency telephones approximately every 20 km (12.5 miles) on main roads. One word of warning: don't break down on a Sunday. Despite the gloomy implication, all is not lost for those who do. Dial 17, wherever you are, and the **125**

police can put you in touch with a garage that will come to your rescue. At a price, of course – so it's wise to take out an international breakdown insurance before leaving home. Always ask for an estimate before authorizing repairs, and expect to pay *TVA* (value-added tax) on top of the cost.

Fuel and oil (*essence; huile*). Fuel is available as *super* (98 octane), *normale* (90 octane), lead free *(sans plomb)* (usually 98, sometimes 95 octane) and diesel *(gas-oil)*. It's customary to give a small tip, particularly if the garage hand checks your tyre pressure. Fuel stations are mostly self-service. On Saturdays it's worth remembering to fill up as many garages are closed on Sundays. Petrol being quite an expensive item, it's advisable to avoid buying it on motorways. It's about 15% cheaper at supermarkets.

Chaussée déformée	Uneven road surface
Déviation	Diversion (detour)
Gravillons	Loose gravel
Péage	Toll
Priorité à droite	Yield to traffic from the right
Ralentir	Slow down
Serrez à droite/à gauche	Keep right/left
driving licence	permis de conduire
car registration papers	carte grise
Are we on the right road for...?	Sommes-nous sur la route de...?
Fill the tank, please.	Le plein, s'il vous plaît.
lead-free/normal/super	sans plomb/normale/super
I've had a breakdown.	Ma voiture est en panne.
There's been an accident.	Il y a eu un accident.

ELECTRIC CURRENT
Although the voltage is the same as that in Britain, an adaptor is necessary as the plugs are different.

EMBASSIES and CONSULATES
Contact your consulate or embassy when in trouble (loss of passport, theft or loss of all your money, problems with the police, after a serious accident). The nearest British and U.S. consulates are in Bordeaux at:

United Kingdom: 15, cours de Verdun, 33081 Bordeaux;
tel. 56 52 28 35.

U.S.A.: 22, cours du Maréchal Foch, 33080 Bordeaux;
tel. 56 52 65 95.

   Citizens of other English-speaking countries should get in touch with their representatives in Paris.

Australia (embassy and consulate): 4, rue Jean-Rey, 75015 Paris;
tel. 16 (1) 40 59 33 00.

Canada (embassy): 35, avenue Montaigne, 75008 Paris;
tel. 16 (1) 47 23 01 01.

Irish Republic (embassy): 12, avenue Foch (enter from 4, rue Rude), 75016 Paris; tel. 16 (1) 45 00 20 87.

New Zealand (embassy-chancellery): 7 ter, rue Léonard-de-Vinci, 75116 Paris; tel. 16 (1) 45 00 24 11.

South Africa (chancellery-consulate): 59, quai d'Orsay, 75007 Paris; tel. 16 (1) 45 55 92 37.

EMERGENCIES (urgence)
You can get assistance anywhere in France by dialling 17 for the police (*police secours*); 18 for the fire brigade (*pompiers*), who also turn out for medical emergencies.

For ambulances, you call the number in the telephone box or the police (*brigade de gendarmes*).

Careful!	**Attention!**	Police!	**Police!**
Fire!	**Au feu!**	Stop, thief!	**Au voleur!**
Help!	**Au secours!**		

Can you help me? **Pouvez-vous m'aider?**

ETIQUETTE

As a friendly hospitable people, tolerant but profoundly French, the Périgourdin don't quite know what to make of this latest invasion – English housebuyers, Dutch tourists and German businessmen.

Although there is some resentment towards wealthy foreigners, in the end good sense gets the upper hand, everyone sees where his interest lies and a good dose of give-and-take calms the unsettled waters.

However, there is a code of ethics for the foreigner: smile, be open and be willing to accept the Périgourdin way of doing things; a little French, however basic, is always appreciated and while tourism keeps the economy afloat, agriculture is the main industry, so farmers do not like being taken for granted or treated as second-class citizens.

G ▬▬▬▬▬▬▬▬▬▬▬▬▬▬▬▬▬▬▬▬▬▬▬▬▬▬

GETTING THERE and AROUND

The nearest international airport for the Dordogne is Bordeaux, linked by scheduled flights to and from London Heathrow, Birmingham, Manchester, Newcastle, Glasgow, Edinburgh and Belfast (to reserve a flight, ring (071) 897 4000). From Bordeaux, coaches (called *cars,* don't get confused) or trains run regularly to Bergerac, Périgueux and Sarlat. To save money reserve a PEX or SUPERPEX fare, payable on booking, which require a minimum stay and carry an alteration or cancellation penalty. Excursion fares stipulate a minimum stay, but there are no other restrictions.

By coach. There are daily departures to Bordeaux from the Victoria Coach Station in London. Although it is a long journey, much is overnight and it's quite an economical and surprisingly comfortable way of getting to the Dordogne. At Bordeaux you change coaches for Sarlat, Bergerac or Périgueux.

By car. To get there rapidly, do the 900-odd km (560 miles) from Calais to Bordeaux by motorway: the A26 from Calais speeds you to Paris, and then take the A10 through to Bordeaux. Note that the toll (*péage*) is expensive, so you may prefer to tackle the latter part of the route on the roads parallel to the motorway or else get off at Saintes and go via Cognac, Angoulême and Brantôme to Périgueux.

By train. From Paris, the *TGV Atlantique* runs to Bordeaux ($1^1/_4$ hours by train to Périgueux), but nowhere in the Dordogne. Therefore, most people opt for the less onerous options such as plane, coach or car. Anyone permanently residing outside France can buy the France-Pass (called France Railpass overseas) which gives unlimited travel for any 4 days to be used within 15 days or else 9 or 16 days to be used within a month, depending on which pass you buy.

HOUSE PURCHASING

Although it's the 'in-thing' to buy a house in the Dordogne, some foreigners do not give it enough thought. Admittedly real bargains are to be had, but at the end of a delightful holiday purchasers are sometimes blind to the realities that await them: property taxes and rates, different French laws, papers to be filled out, getting phones or drains installed, most of this having to be dealt with in French. Many of the houses are isolated, often in hamlets or villages. The villagers, farmers for the most part, sometimes view this 'invasion' with a certain apprehension and even (if they feel outnumbered) irritation. On the other hand, some people feel that they have found their nirvana. When choosing your agency, one precaution is to see if it belongs to the FNAIM (*Fédération Nationale d'Agents Immobiliers*).

LANGUAGE

The French are inordinately proud of their language and handle it with enviable skill and wit at all levels of society. Inevitably, a foreigner may stutter and stumble, but that's far better as far as the French are concerned than not making an effort. Never take an understanding of English for granted but congratulate the person that does speak it – a little encouragement will make them better disposed to help you. In hotels, restaurants, campsites and *Syndicats d'Initiative*, you will just about always find someone who can speak English.

The French spoken in the Dordogne already has the warm, rich intonations of the Midi, without its 'twang'. In fact, the Périgord dubs itself *midi moins le quart* (playing on the *midi*'s double meaning of south and noon).

Goodbye.	**Au revoir.**
You're welcome.	**Je vous en prie.**
Speak slowly, please.	**Parlez lentement, s'il vous plaît.**
I didn't understand.	**Je n'ai pas compris.**

MEDICAL CARE (See also EMERGENCIES)

Make sure your health insurance policy covers illness or accident while on holiday. If not, ask your insurance representative, motoring association or travel agent about special holiday insurance plans.

Visitors from EC countries with corresponding health insurance facilities are entitled to medical and hospital treatment under the French social security system. Before leaving home, ensure that you are eligible and have the appropriate forms required to obtain this benefit in case of need. Doctors who belong to the French social security system (*médecins conventionnés*) charge the minimum rate.

If you're taken ill or have a toothache, your hotel receptionist can probably recommend an English-speaking doctor or dentist; otherwise ask at the *Syndicat d'Initiative* or, in an emergency, the *gendarmerie*.

Chemists (*pharmacies*) display green crosses. Staff are helpful in dealing with minor ailments and can recommend a nurse (*infirmière*) if you need injections or other special care. In towns throughout the Dordogne, there'll be a chemist on duty at night on a rota system (*service de garde*). The name and address of the duty chemist is displayed in the window of other pharmacies. You can also get it from the *gendarmerie* or the local papers. *Sud-Ouest* lists chemists and doctors on call (*pharmaciens/médecins de garde*).

MONEY MATTERS

Currency. The French *franc* (abbreviated F or FF) is divided into 100 *centimes* (ct.).

● Coins: 5, 10, 20, 50 ct.; 1, 2, 5, 10 F.

● Banknotes: 20, 50, 100, 200, 500 F.

For currency restrictions, see CUSTOMS and ENTRY FORMALITIES.

Banks and currency exchange (Also see OPENING HOURS). Local tourist offices *may* change money outside banking hours at the official bank rate. Take your passport when you go to change money or traveller's cheques. Your hotel may also come to the rescue, though you'll get a less favourable rate of exchange. The same applies to foreign currency or traveller's cheques changed in stores, boutiques or restaurants.

Credit cards are used in an increasing number of hotels, restaurants, shops and service stations, as well as for obtaining money from cash dispensers (*distributeurs automatiques*).

Traveller's cheques and Eurocheques are widely accepted throughout France. Outside town, it's preferable to have some ready cash with you, especially for paying for petrol.

Sales tax. A value-added tax *(TVA)* is imposed on almost all goods and services. In hotels and restaurants, this is accompanied by a service charge.

Visitors from non-EC countries will be refunded the *TVA* on larger purchases. Ask the sales assistant for the requisite form, to be filled out and handed to French customs on departure.

Where's the nearest bank/currency exchange office?	**Où se trouve la banque/lebureau de change la/le plus proche?**
I want to change some pounds/dollars.	**Je voudrais changer des livres sterling/des dollars.**
Do you accept traveller's cheques/this credit card?	**Acceptez-vous les chèques de voyage/cette carte de crédit?**

NEWSPAPERS and MAGAZINES (journaux; magazines)

During the tourist season you can be pretty certain of getting major British and other European newspapers and news magazines on publication day or the following morning. The Paris edition of the *International Herald Tribune* is available at main newsagents in resorts and larger towns. A most thoughtful and interesting review in English comes out five times a year, the *Dordogne Telegraph*, with articles helping not only to get the feel of the area but to understand French life and to know what is going on. In the local daily, *Sud Ouest*, there is half a page in English (and French) devoted to sports and cultural activities going on that day in the Dordogne.

OPENING HOURS (heures d'ouverture)

Banks tend to open weekdays from 9 a.m. to 5 p.m. (many closing for lunch from noon until 2 a.m.) and close either on Saturdays (main towns) or Mondays. All banks close on major national or regional holidays and most close early on the day preceding a public holiday.

Main post offices are open weekdays 8 a.m. to 7 p.m., Saturdays until noon. Post offices in smaller towns usually close for lunch from noon until 2 or 2.30 p.m., as well as shutting for the day at 5 or 6 p.m.

Groceries, bakeries and food shops are open Monday to Saturday 7 a.m. to 7 p.m. Food shops are often open on Sunday mornings – bakeries, butchers, *charcuteries,* in particular, but also some supermarkets. Lunch-time closing, from 12.30 to 2 p.m., is the norm for small shops.

Other shops are generally open Tuesday to Saturday 9 or 9.30 a.m. to 6.30 or 7 p.m., closing Monday morning or all day.

Museums, châteaux, caves and monuments are usually open 10 a.m. to 5.30 p.m. They're often closed on Tuesday, but not always. Unfortunately, you simply have to check hours and availability before going.

P

PHOTOGRAPHY

Film is somewhat expensive in France. If you can, buy your films in Britain before you leave. Photography is not allowed in the caves – if you try to sneak a camera in you could face a heavy fine.

PLANNING YOUR BUDGET

The following list will give you an idea of what to expect in the Dordogne. As prices vary considerably and rise inexorably, they must be considered approximate.

Babysitters. 15–20 F/hour (student, to be negotiated).

133

Bicycle/Scooter Hire. 75 F half a day for a mountain bike, 100 F a day, 515 F a week ; normal bicycle (*vélo randonnée*) 50 F half a day, 60 F a day, 310 F a week. Returnable deposit around 500 F. Scooter 200 F a day, 840 F a week.

Boat trips. Bergerac adults 35 F, children 20 F for a 1-hour trip in a *gabare*; Beynac 45 minutes-trip 30 F (children up to twelve 15 F).

Camp site. 2-star site: 2 adults, 2 children over seven (under sevens or fives are usually free), car/caravan, electricity and local tax 50–65 F.

Car hire. International company, *TVA* included: *Peugeot 309* 268 F a day plus 3.88 F per km, 3,160 F per week with unlimited mileage; *Renault 21* 365 F a day plus 4.85 F per km, 4,440 F a week with un-limited mileage.

Entertainment and culture. Cinema 30 F, discothèque 80–100 F (drink sometimes included), festival concert 100–170 F, sound-and-light spectacle (Rocamadour) 80–115 F, commentated tours (Sarlat) 20 F (students 11 F), leisure park 45 F (whole day, general entry), helicopter ride (30 minutes) 600 F per person.

Hotels. Double room in hotels 2-star 280–400 F, 3-star 300–500 F, 4-star 400 F and up; *chambre d'hôtes* 150–250 F.

Meals. Breakfast 20–40 F, lunch or dinner (3–5 course *menu,* medi-um establishment) 75–250 F, luxury establishment 250–450 F (with-out wine); dish of the day (lunch time) 50–65 F; bottle of Bergerac/Coteaux de Quercy 40–60 F, Pécharmant 60–100 F, half-litre *pichet* of wine 25–30 F, mineral water 15–20 F, coffee 6–14 F.

Museums and Caves. Le Bugue 20 F, usually 22–45 F (Lascaux II with Le Thot), guide 3–5 F tip per person expected.

Shopping. Bread (*baguette)* 4 F, butter 8–14 F, *foie gras de canard entier* 200 g (portions for 4) 114 F, *confits de canard* (2 portions) 57 F, gift basket around 550 F, *rillettes de canard* 200 g 22 F, bottle of Bergerac 12 F, Pécharmant 22 F.

Sports activities. Canoe hire (3–4 hours) 60–100 F per person (children 40–80 F) includes mini-bus return to departure point, 2 days 180 F, week 450 F (kayak slightly more); horse-riding 70 F 1-hour lesson, 600 F 10-hour excursion, week 2,700 F; horse and carriage 200 F per person per day (with driver); accompanied walks half-day 50 F, full day 70 F per person; pedalo hire 10 F half-hour.

POLICE

In cities and larger towns, you'll see the blue-uniformed *police municipale;* they are the local police force who direct traffic, keep order and investigate crime.

Outside the main towns are the *gendarmes;* they wear blue trousers and black jackets with white belts and are responsible for traffic and crime investigation. They are usually pleasant, helpful and efficient, but not many speak English.

POST OFFICES

French post offices display a sign with a stylized bluebird and/or the words *Postes et Télécommunications*, *P&T* or *La Poste*. Queues can be quite long. Depending on where it is or whether it is simply a tiny *agence postale* or a main office, hours vary.

In addition to the normal mail service, you can make local or long-distance telephone calls, buy *télécartes* (phone cards) and receive or send money at any post office.

Poste restante (general delivery). If you don't know where you'll be staying, you can have your mail addressed to you in any town c/o *Poste restante, Poste centrale*. You can collect it on presentation of your passport for a small fee. Post can be sluggish in the summer months.

Telegrams. Telegrams are on their way out. Local post offices still accept inland and overseas telegrams, however, and you can also **135**

dictate one over the phone (dial 14). A telegram can be handed in to a post office up to ten days before you want it sent.

express (special delivery)	**par exprès**
airmail	**par avion**
registered	**en recommandé**
Have you any mail for...?	**Avez-vous du courrier pour...?**

PUBLIC HOLIDAYS (jours fériés)

January 1	*Jour de l'An*	New Year's Day
May 1	*Fête du Travail*	Labour Day
May 8	*Fête de la Victore 1945*	Victory Day
July 14	*Fête nationale*	Bastille Day
August 15	*Assomption*	Assumption
November 1	*Toussaint*	All Saints' Day
November 11	*Armistice*	Armistice Day (1918)
December 25	*Noël*	Christmas Day
Moveable dates:	*Lundi de Pâques*	Easter Monday
	Ascension	Ascension
	Lundi de Pentecôte	Whit Monday

In France, school holidays vary from region to region but, as elsewhere, resorts tend to fill up in the summer. In general, children's summer holidays begin in late June and finish in September. August can be appallingly crowded in big centres.

Are you open tomorrow?	**Est-ce que vous ouvrez demain?**

PUBLIC TRANSPORT

Although public transport is available in most towns, it is not advisable to use the local buses or trains for getting to the major sites as this will cut into your sightseeing time. You are nearly always better off using a car or else, in town, walking.

RESTAURANTS (See also the HOTEL/RESTAURANT SECTION)

In bigger towns, you'll have a choice between gourmet restaurants, large family-sized *brasseries* or the more intimate little *bistrot* and cafés for a cheaper snack.

The *menu* can consist of anything from three or four courses to six or even more. If you're daunted by the *menu*, choose à la carte, but be aware that the same item is far more expensive than on the *menu*. The word *carte* means 'menu' – a *menu* is the suggested meal for the day at a fixed price, balanced, often regional and usually good value for money.

It's considered good form to leave a personal tip for the waiter, beyond any formal one in the bill, *if* he or she has done all within their power to make your meal enjoyable. No obligation – simply a gesture. Look out for *service non compris* or *en sus* ('service not included').

To help you order...

Waiter/Waitress	**Garçon/Mademoiselle (Madame)**
Can we have a table please?	**Pouvons-nous avoir une table?**
The menu, please.	**La carte, s'il vous plaît.**
Do you have a set menu ?	**Avez-vous un menu du jour?**
I'd like a/an/some …	**J'aimerais …**

butter	**du beurre**	meat	**de la viande**
bread	**du pain**	milk	**du lait**
chips	**des frites**	mineral water	**de l'eau minérale**
coffee	**un café**	sugar	**du sucre**
fish	**du poisson**	tea	**du thé**
fruit	**un fruit**	(iced)water	**de l'eau (glacée)**
ice-cream	**une glace**	wine	**du vin**

137

...and read the menu

agneau	lamb	**gigot**	leg of lamb
ail	garlic	**haricots verts**	string beans
andouillette	tripe sausage	**jambon**	ham
artichauts	artichokes	**melon**	melon
bœuf	beef	**moules**	mussels
canard	duck	**moutarde**	mustard
carottes	carrots	**nouilles**	noodles
cervelle	brain	**oignons**	onions
champignons	mushrooms	**petits pois**	peas
chou	cabbage	**poireaux**	leeks
chou-fleur	cauliflower	**pommes**	apples
concombre	cucumber	**potage**	soup
côtelettes	chops, cutlets	**poulet**	chicken
crevettes	shrimps	**raisin**	grapes
endive	endive	**riz**	rice
épinards	spinach	**rognons**	kidneys
flageolets	beans	**saucisse**	sausage
foie	liver	**saucisson**	dried sausage
fraises	strawberries	**saumon**	salmon
framboises	raspberries	**thon**	tuna
frites	chips (French fries)	**truffes**	truffles
		veau	veal
fruits de mer	seafood	**volaille**	poultry

TELEPHONE (téléphone)

More and more phone boxes only take *télécartes* (from post offices or tobacconists) for 50 or 120 units. Coin-operated phones take 50-centime, 1-franc, 2-franc and 5-franc coins.

To make an international call, dial 19 and wait for a continuous tone before dialling the rest of the number.

Australia	19 61	South Africa	19 27
Canada	19 1	United Kingdom	19 44
New Zealand	19 64	United States	19 1

TIME DIFFERENCES

France keeps to Central European Time (GMT+1). Summer time (GMT+2) comes into force between late March and the end of September. The following chart gives summer time differences.

New York	London	**Paris**	Sydney	Auckland
6 a.m.	11 a.m.	**noon**	8 p.m.	10 p.m.

What time is it? **Quelle heure est-il?**

TIPPING

A little tip can go a long way in the Dordogne, all the more so now that the practice is dying out as a result of inexorable inflation. In the main, the tip has been incorporated into restaurant prices. Except for museum and cave guides who depend on it, a tip is given for a particularly appreciated service.

Hotel porter, per bag	4–5 F
Hotel maid, per week	50–100 F
Lavatory attendant	2 F
Waiter	5–10% (optional)
Taxi driver	10–15%
Hairdresser/Barber	15% (gen. incl.)
Tour guide	10%

139

TOILETS

Regular visitors to France will notice that remarkable progress has been made in recent years. Toilets are for the most part modern, fully equipped and have wash basins and soap. If you use those in a café, you should at least buy a coffee (or a postcard, if it's also a tobacconists). There are still, of course, hiccups in the system. At the other end of the scale, you may still occasionally come upon 'footprints' (*à la turque*), the door may not close (the lock is sometimes the light switch as well) and toilet paper may be found wanting.

Where are the toilets, please?   **Où sont les toilettes, s'il vous plaît?**

TOURIST INFORMATION OFFICES

The local tourist office – the *Syndicat d'Initiative* (S.I.) or *Office de Tourisme* – is usually situated close to the centre of town or the railway station. Hours vary, but in the summer most tourist offices open every day, except Sunday, from 9 or 9.30 a.m. until noon or 1 p.m., and again from 1 or 2 p.m. until 6 or 6.30 p.m. Out of season, hours are limited and many *Syndicats d'Initiative* close.

There are French National Tourist Offices in the following English-speaking countries:

Australia	Kindersley House, 33 Bligh Street, Sydney, NSW 2000; tel. (2) 231 5244
Canada	1981 Avenue McGill College, Suite 490, Esso Tower, Montreal, Que. H3 A2 W9; tel. (514) 288 4264
	1, Dundas Street West, Suite 2405, Box 8, Toronto, Ont. M5 G1 Z3; tel. (416) 593 4717
South Africa	Carlton Centre, 10th Floor, P.O. Box 1081, Johannesburg 2000; tel. (11) 331 9252
UK	178 Piccadilly, London W1V 0AL; tel. (071) 493 6594

USA	610 Fifth Avenue, New York, NY 10020; tel. (212) 757 1125
	645 North Michigan Avenue, Suite 630, Chicago, Illinois 60611; tel. (312) 337 6301
	9401 Wilshire Boulevard, Beverly Hills, California 90212; tel. (213) 272 2661
	1 Hallidie Plaza, San Francisco, California 94102; tel. (415) 986 4174
	World Trade Center, N103, 2050 Stemmons Freeway, P.O. Box 58610, Dallas, Texas 75258; tel. (214) 742 7011

If you can manage a little French, Radio France provides information on 99 Mhz, at 7.15 and 8.45 a.m. as well as 12.45 and 6.45 p.m., on the situation regarding campsites and hotels generally, as well as the day's events.

WATER

Although tap water is safe to drink (fine for brushing your teeth, etc.) it is not particularly tasty so you're better off buying a bottle of still *(sans gaz)* or fizzy *(avec gaz)* mineral water.

YOUTH HOSTELS (Auberge de Jeunesse)

The Dordogne has three youth hostels (at Périgueux, Sarlat and Saint-Barthélemy-de-Bellegarde), and the Lot has two (at Figeac and Cahors). Most offer standard amenities, but none are big (Sarlat has 40 beds, Périgueux only 16), so it's best to ring and check if there's room. To get full information, ask for the free guide to all French youth hostels available from the Fédération Unie des Auberges de Jeunesse (FUAJ), 27, rue Pagol, 75018 Paris; tel. 16 (1) 46 07 00 01. **141**

Index

Where there is more than one set of page references, the one in bold type refers to the main entry. Definite articles, such as *Le*, *La* and *Les*, follow the rest of the name.